Advance Praise for *Mad Travelers*

"Dave Seminara has written a gripping detective story that is also a fascinating history of, and meditation on, the powerful attraction of travel."

—THOMAS SWICK, author of *The Joys of Travel: And Stories That Illuminate Them*

"A revolutionary insight into the mindset of the modern traveler. Full of fascinating stories of adventure that don't hold back on the darker aspects of the reality of wanderlust."

—LEVISON WOOD, author of *Walking the Nile*

"This madcap, hard-to-put-down tale gets to the heart of the big question: why do we travel? And why are some people so wild with wanderlust? Dave Seminara's wonderfully written tome detailing the untamed lust for travel is a superb story to get lost in."

—DAVID FARLEY, author of *An Irreverent Curiosity: In Search of the Church's Strangest Relic in Italy's Oddest Town*

"A fascinating account of an extreme, obsessive travel subculture and a brilliant young con man who fleeced its members while masquerading as an upper crust English billionaire. This book is essential reading for anyone with terminal wanderlust (like me) and those who puzzle over our psychology."

—RICHARD GRANT, author of *American Nomads*

"Dave Seminara, himself an esteemed collector of passport stamps, has assembled a tale almost too delicious to be true. Part globe-hopping adventure, part detective story, and part examination of the murky world of obsessive travelers, this book reads like a missing season of *Parts Unknown* in which Anthony Bourdain visits a dozen Fyre Festivals."

—MARK ADAMS, author of *Turn Right at Machu Picchu: Rediscovering the Lost City One Step at a Time*

"This is a book about the crackheads of travel. The obsessives. The compulsive. The people with a *problem*. Normal people take their vacations in Cancun. Or Italy. Or Tahiti. And then there are the weirdos who pencil in a week in Mogadishu. Or a grueling trip to an obscure island in the Chukchi Sea. Seminara's tale isn't about geography. It's about the obsession that drives people to the ends of the Earth."

—J. MAARTEN TROOST, author of *The Sex Lives of Cannibals: Adrift in the Equatorial Pacific*

"*Mad Travelers* is a strange and delightful tale. William Baaekeland, a swindler and world traveler extraordinaire with an honest case of wanderlust, is masterfully dissected. By the end, I was examining my own rambles with a fresh perspective. Take this book on your next long flight—preferably to someplace way, way off the beaten path."

—NOAH STRYKER, author of *Birding Without Borders: An Obsession, a Quest, and the Biggest Year in the World*

Also by Dave Seminara

Footsteps of Federer: A Fan's Pilgrimage
Across 7 Swiss Cantons in 10 Acts

MAD TRAVELERS

A TALE OF WANDERLUST, GREED
AND THE QUEST TO REACH THE ENDS OF THE EARTH

DAVE SEMINARA

Post Hill
PRESS

A POST HILL PRESS BOOK
ISBN: 978-1-64293-858-6
ISBN (eBook): 978-1-64293-859-3

Mad Travelers:
A Tale of Wanderlust, Greed and the Quest to Reach the Ends of the Earth
© 2021 by Dave Seminara
All Rights Reserved

Cover design by Chad Lowe

This is a true story. Most of the characters are identified here using their real names. In a few cases, the author has elected to change names of parties that didn't grant authorized interviews for use in this book.

Post Hill Press
New York • Nashville
posthillpress.com

Published in the United States of America
1 2 3 4 5 6 7 8 9 10

For Carmen and Joanne Seminara, my biggest fans.

CONTENTS

◇◇◇◇◇◇◇

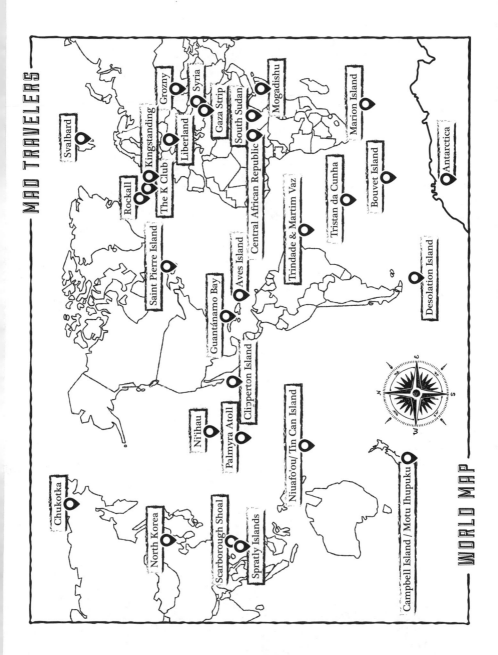

MAD TRAVELERS

WORLD MAP

Svalbard

Grozny
Kingstanding
Rockall
The K Club
Liberland
Syria
Gaza Strip
South Sudan
Central African Republic
Mogadishu
Marion Island

Antarctica

Saint Pierre Island
Aves Island
Trindade & Martim Vaz
Tristan da Cunha
Bouvet Island
Desolation Island

Guantánamo Bay
Clipperton Island

Ni'ihau
Palmyra Atoll
Niuafo'ou/ Tin Can Island

Chukotka
North Korea
Scarborough Shoal
Spratly Islands
Campbell Island / Motu Ihupuku

Wherever my travels may lead,
paradise is where I am.

—Voltaire

CHAPTER 1

◇◇◇◇◇◇◇

Extreme Travel
Rock Star

Our battered suitcases were piled on the sidewalk again;
we had longer ways to go. But no matter, the road is life.

—JACK KEROUAC

When William S. Baekeland's name first popped into my Gmail inbox on October 12, 2015, it felt like an encounter with an elusive celebrity or a brush with a member of the British royal family. I had heard a lot about the brainy and daring young billionaire explorer from other prolific travelers I profiled, most for a BBC series called Travel Pioneers. The series gave me a chance to meet some of the world's greatest travelers—men who had been to not just every country in the world, but nearly every speck on the map. Their quest is to get to the hard-to-reach, virtually unvisited places at the ends of the earth and young William was the lad who was getting them where they wanted to go, or at least was promising to try. How could I resist the opportunity to profile a twenty-one-year-old billionaire whose travel resume floored even these hyper-well-traveled men?

Months before, I pitched a television production company on making a TV series about the world's top travelers and they paid me a trifling sum for the rights to my idea, with the promise of significantly more if a network bought the show they developed. But a problem emerged as they began to interview the travelers whom I recommended: the world's top travelers were all older, straight white guys, and many of them were retired.

"The networks want stars who are in the right demo," said my contact at the production company, an industry veteran. "In order to sell this, we need younger travelers. And women."

The fact that these men were venturing to fascinating, forbidden places that even geography buffs would struggle to locate on a map was apparently irrelevant. The networks wanted a *Survivor* cast: young multiracial people who look great in bathing suits, at least one person with a Southern drawl, and so on.

I doubled back to my network of extreme travelers in search of younger, more demographically interesting country collectors, and several made the same recommendation: William S. Baekeland. Here are some of the adjectives the country collectors used to describe him: rich, brilliant, genius, incredible, wise, remarkable. One prominent extreme traveler said in an interview that he was destined to become the world's most traveled person.

I relayed his bio to the production company and they were sold on him before they even heard his voice. What's not to like about a handsome young billionaire with a posh British accent and time on his hands to travel to far-flung corners of the planet?

In that first email, William told me that he was working on completing the travel destination lists of two prominent clubs—the Travelers' Century Club (TCC) and Most Traveled People (MTP), as well as his own "Baekelist" of twelve thousand world highlights he developed.

"Many of the places I wish to reach are hard, inaccessible and utterly remote," he wrote. He continued:

> To get there, you have to find your own way there. For example, I am really keen on islands. Many have no sort of scheduled service or even occasional cruises. I have to charter my own yacht or ship. At the moment for example, I am working on getting my Antarctic continent and sub Antarctic islands['] full circumnavigation by ship worked out. Each island requires permits and planning—it is a large undertaking to get to many places.

Baekeland politely concluded that he looked forward to speaking with me, wishing me "all the best." But he broke multiple telephone appointments and then did the same to the production company. Travelers told me that he probably bailed because, as a billionaire, he liked to keep a low profile, and, in any case, had nothing to promote on television.

I concluded that Baekeland had better things to do with his time. After all, he was a busy young man who apparently had billions at his disposal. By twenty-three, William Baekeland had already seen more of the world than most people manage in a life-time. He had visited 163 countries, and his goal was to see the thirty others that he hadn't been to. Then he'd focus on visiting every country twice. Baekeland's passion was finding ways to get to the world's most challenging destinations—dangerous places, disputed territories, and, most of all, remote or officially off-limits islands few could spot on a world map.

Rather than mingling with backpackers his own age on the beaches of Ibiza or Santorini, he frequently traveled with extreme travelers more than twice his age. He was the godfather of country collecting in that he worked tirelessly to help get the world's top travelers to the hardest-to-get-to geographic oddities on the lists of the three biggest travel clubs: MTP, TCC, and a third called NomadMania/The Best Traveled (TBT).

Baekeland wasn't in it for the money. William played the harpsichord and was writing a book about Norwegian Antarctica. And he wasn't boastful—unlike most young globetrotters, he didn't have a website or a blog to document his extensive travels. But everyone in the tight-knit community of extreme travel, including several men whom I profiled, heard that he was a billionaire who had inherited his fortune from his great-grandfather, Leo Baekeland, considered the father of the plastics industry for his invention of Bakelite, an inexpensive, nonflammable, and versatile plastic, in 1907.

Time magazine listed Leo as one of the hundred most important figures of the twentieth century, but the family also had a spell of tabloid infamy after his death. In 1972, Barbara Baekeland, the ex-wife of Brooks Baekeland, grandson of Leo, was stabbed to death with a kitchen knife by her son, Tony. According to the book, *Savage Grace: The True Story of Fatal Relations in a Rich and Famous*

American Family, Tony was gay or bisexual and his mother hired prostitutes and even slept with him in failed bids to convert him to heterosexuality.

William never mentioned the incident, and, in any case, his credibility among elite travelers couldn't have been higher. Men who traveled almost everywhere would be stumped when, in his posh, upper-crust British accent, he would name-drop places like Kapingamarangi, a forgotten atoll in the Federated States of Micronesia, or Trindade and Martin Vaz, a stunning archipelago in the southern Atlantic Ocean that serves as a garrison for the Brazilian Navy.

He led these extreme travelers on expeditions he planned using his extensive diplomatic and maritime industry contacts to off-limits islands in the Pacific, like Palmyra, and to war-torn countries like the Central African Republic and South Sudan. William had no occupation, save for managing some of his family's lands in Scotland, and was decades younger than most of the other top travelers, who spent a lifetime building the kind of travel resume he had accumulated seemingly overnight.

His 2016 Christmas card is illustrative of his jet-setting lifestyle. It included a review of his "year in travel," documented through a seventy-nine-photo slideshow featuring his seventh around-the-world journey, his "pioneering" adventures crossing Russia's Northeast Passage on an icebreaker ship, landing near the summit of Mount Everest in a helicopter, and a host of other adventures from the forbidden Hawaiian island of Niihau to a Namibian ghost town and beyond.

A vegetarian—bone-thin and handsome—he looked and dressed like someone who might be rejected from a Brooks Brothers catalog audition for being a bit too skinny and earnest. Baekeland oozed sincerity and people of all nationalities found him to be personable and good company.

In his Christmas card, Baekeland described 2016 as an "indescribably bad and difficult year." In August, his sister Muguette died in New York. Two months later, he wrote, he lost his sister Ariadne to "weariness of life" (suicide). William asserted that his intensive travel schedule had "helped significantly with all of the challenges faced during this past year."

He kept traveling, and, in February 2017, while on a trip to Antarctica, Baekeland's father died, and he couldn't get to the funeral. Other travelers said he was inconsolable, but the losses didn't stop him from making trips to the Pacific island of Clipperton, the Central African Republic, East Timor, war-torn Syria, and Libya. He was closing in on his goal of visiting all 193 countries (as defined by the United Nations), and planned to visit his final target—Serbia—along with his mother, Lady Violette Baekeland, in October 2017 for an elite extreme traveler conference where they were set to become the first mother-son team to have visited every country in the world.

Baekeland and Lady Violette didn't turn up in Liberland, a micro-nation that is essentially an unclaimed island in the Danube that straddles the Serb/Croat border. But many of the world's top travelers attended the conference, and as they began to share stories and compare notes on a flurry of trips that William had recently cancelled, it became clear that the young billionaire owed a number of travelers tens or perhaps hundreds of thousands of dollars.

Discretion and some degree of secrecy are the norm within this small community of extreme world travelers. Many had relied on William to get them to some of the world's hardest-to-reach destinations while maintaining discretion regarding these trips, which helped some gain a competitive advantage over their rivals. But once communication lines opened, and the founder of one of the leading clubs for top travelers started digging into Baekeland's story, some began to doubt him.

Could a young man who barely needed to shave dupe a collection of the world's best-traveled people? In early 2018, I became obsessed with untangling this question. It seemed like the ultimate example of the perils of wanderlust—his clients were desperate to get to the ends of the earth and were willing to do almost anything to hit their targets.

Was William a con man or just a kid with incurable wanderlust who had gotten in over his head while trying to fund his travel ambitions? I needed to find out.

CHAPTER 2

◇◇◇◇◇◇◇◇

Passage to Bouvet Island

*For once you have tasted flight, you will walk the
earth with your eyes turned skywards, for there you
have been and there you will long to return.*

—LEONARDO DA VINCI

F ew travel agents would recommend a thirty-five-day South
Atlantic Ocean cruise with frigid, spectacularly remote ports
of call like Bouvet Island, an uninhabited subantarctic volcanic
spec on the map that is considered the most remote island in the
world. Seasoned travelers pay $10,000 each for a shared cabin or
$15,000 and up for private cabins that are far from luxurious. There
are no swimming pools, no spa treatments, no limbo contests, or
casinos on board. And since the weather and seas are frequently
violent and capricious in this part of the world, the operator—
Oceanwide Expeditions—won't guarantee that it'll call on any of
the advertised ports of call: the South Shetland Islands, the South

Sandwich Islands, Tristan da Cunha, Gough Island, Bouvet, and St. Helena, which was Napoleon's place of exile. Even in calm seas, due to the distances involved, passengers spend nearly the entire cruise on board the ship.

Bouvet Island

Any of these factors would be deal breakers for ordinary travelers, but not for extreme travelers like William Baekeland and about sixty other seasoned travelers who were on Oceanwide Expeditions' *Ortelius* as it bobbed in 80-mph winds near Bouvet Island on April 5, 2015. They were thrilled by the possibility of landing on the world's most isolated island. For them, wanderlust is like a divine calling that is best indulged, not fought, and a landing on this holy grail of extreme travel would give them bragging rights akin to a big game hunter who had bagged a lion.

Obsessive travelers want to go "everywhere," but they do not agree on what that term means. Some members of the travel clubs, like Jorge Sánchez—a Spaniard who dropped out of school at fourteen and has traveled the world while intermittently working odd jobs—believe that peculiar, uninhabited islands like Bouvet shouldn't count as places to visit.

But it does and many of the world's top travelers were with young William Baekeland on the *Ortelius*.

Dominique Laurent (left) and William

Their ranks included Chicago-area residents Bob Bonifas and Don Parrish, then ranked number one and number two on MTP, Frank Wigand Grosse-Oetringhaus, a German man ranked number four on TBT, but who is, according to his own calculation, the world's best-traveled person, his Filipino partner, Teodoro Murallon, and other top travelers like Dominique Laurent, a retired French financial manager, and Harry Mitsidis, the British-Greek founder of NomadMania, which ranks him as the world's most traveled person.

Mitsidis, forty-three at the time, was probably the second-youngest person on the ship, even though he was old enough to be William's father. Born in London to a Greek father and South African mother, Mitsidis had already visited every country in the world by forty and one of his goals was to visit every country in the world twice by fifty. In his bio, Harry says that he has three master's degrees and speaks eleven languages, including four fluently. Mitsidis was once a lecturer in quality management and leadership but apparently has the means to travel for most of the year. He told me that he owns properties that he rents out, and also has a home in the UK, but he essentially lives the life of a nomad.

At least one person on the ship—Artemy Lebedev, an eccentric Russian blogger who was then ranked number twenty-nine on TBT—felt intimidated by the unique collection of leading travelers. In a podcast interview with Ric Gazarian, the host of a show called *Counting Countries*, he likened himself to a shark that required constant movement to live and "feel happiness." But he felt threatened in these waters.

"We were like a bunch of superheroes all put in one place on this ship," he said. "Imagine I'm Spiderman and have Superman sitting at the table next to me. That's uncomfortable."

Among these travel superstars, William, then twenty-two, stood out on a small ship where most passengers were in their sixties, seventies, and eighties. On a boat where there was little to do but socialize, most were naturally curious to know his story. How did this young man have the cash to pay considerably more for his single cabin?

And how did he have the time to spend thirty-five days on a cruise to such obscure places? Though he was young, travelers say that William acted much older than his age. And though he never boasted about his family background, a German traveler on board the ship spread the word that young William was a Baekeland heir.

©Dominique Laurent

Before long, everyone in the tight-knit group of country collectors on board had heard the news that there was a young aristocratic billionaire on the ship. William didn't have to say much—most figured that any young person on such an exotic trip, and in a more expensive single cabin to boot, had to be extravagantly wealthy. And he sounded the part.

"He had that beautiful British diction," said one top traveler who was there. "He sounded upper crust."

Harry Mitsidis would later recollect in a *Counting Countries* podcast that William's knowledge of geography was so encyclopedic that he could name-drop preposterously obscure places, like Kapingamarangi.

"By the end of the 35-day trip, many were in awe of William, who, despite his shy start, was truly interested in becoming a great traveler and 'seeing it all,' as he put it," Harry would write in a November 2017 NomadMania newsletter.

Named after Abraham Ortelius, a Flemish cartographer who in 1570 published the first modern world atlas, *Theatrum Orbis Terrarum* or *Theatre of the World*, the ship served as a special purpose vessel for the Russian Academy of Sciences and was well equipped for the icy waters of the South Atlantic. The experienced Russian nautical crew assured anxious passengers that they'd make every attempt to help them achieve their goal of stepping foot on Bouvet. But it was already autumn in the Southern Hemisphere and the fierce winds rendered their prospects dicey at best.

Bouvet is a nineteen-square-mile dependency of Norway, 90 percent covered in glaciers and about a thousand miles away from the nearest populated land mass—tiny Tristan da Cunha, a British Overseas Territory with just 262 inhabitants. In a September 2016 interview on the *Counting Countries* podcast, William said that he had always wanted to visit the place since it was the most remote island in the world.

"It was a completely surreal experience finally seeing it because I had thought about it for so long," he said.

There wasn't much for Baekeland to see that he couldn't make out from the deck of the ship, but according to the travel clubs, seeing a place from a boat or a plane doesn't count as a legitimate visit one can tick off toward ranking points. A few top travelers, like Don Parrish, were on the same voyage the year before when the seas had also been too ferocious to allow passengers to visit Bouvet.

Mega-traveler John Clouse, once considered the world's most traveled person, had gotten close to Bouvet twice before, but were foiled by nasty weather each time.

David Langan, a fifty-seven-year-old Irish extreme traveler, once swallowed "half the sea" trying to reach out and touch Rockall—essentially a big uninhabited rock of an island 270 miles off the coast of Ireland that would later become a target for Baekeland and others.

"You have to jump into the water from a Zodiac and the tide brings you against the island," he recalled. "I was holding onto the moss for dear life, looking for some steps to grab onto. I was frightened. It was dangerous. I don't recommend it at all."

Langan says that Bouvet is to extreme travelers as Mount Everest is to climbers. "People would kill their mother to land there."

Charles Veley, a software developer in his fifties who founded MTP, was on the same trip years before. According to a profile in *Washingtonian* magazine, Veley embarked on a time-consuming and risky trip to get to Bouvet in order to dethrone Clouse as the "World's Most Traveled Man" in *The Guinness Book of World Records*. Veley spent seventy-two days on a ship with sailors and military personnel dispatched to Bouvet by South Africa's National Antarctic Programme in order to fix equipment at a weather station on the island. He had to leave his wife and one-month-old baby at home to make the journey.

Their vessel got close to Bouvet's shore but they had to land on the island in a helicopter piloted by the South African Air Force in fifty-knot winds. Veley had a couple hours to snap a few photos and take a quick look around. There wasn't much to see but it was a triumph of will and he had bragging rights. He later said "the experience was on par with witnessing the birth of [his] child."

On the fourteenth day of the *Ortelius*'s thirty-day voyage across the Atlantic to Cape Verde, the ship lingered near Bouvet overnight in similarly windy conditions. The following day, the seas were still far too rough, scuttling any possibility of a landing. The mood on board turned gloomier than the weather. Don Parrish recounted:

> I was repeating the whole trip just to go to Bouvet and it failed. [As we approached Bouvet] I was on pins and needles like everyone else. I talked to the crew and it was clear that there are many ways to fail—it could be the tide, the swell, the wave action. The weather looked like a spooky movie, and I knew we wouldn't make a landing.

Oceanwide Expeditions had a schedule to keep and on April 6 the *Ortelius* circumnavigated Bouvet Island and moved on. Parrish and the others were disappointed but extreme travelers are accustomed to facing adversity in getting to the ends of the earth. It had been nine years since anyone had successfully landed on Bouvet.

"Failure is not unusual," Parrish said. "People fail trying to get to places like this. Here is my test for top travelers, tell me all the places you've failed to get to. The people who have the longest lists, those are the top travelers."

Days later, Baekeland floated a plan to a key group of motivated travelers on board the ship to return to Bouvet later in the year on a private yacht. The *Ortelius* was a repositioning cruise and April wasn't an ideal time to visit. William said that they should return on their own in December or January when the weather would be favorable and they wouldn't be at the mercy of a commercial ship's tight timetable. Dominique Laurent, sixty-seven, a retired financial manager from Paris then ranked number forty-three on TBT, was one of the disappointed travelers who was receptive to William's plan.

"He led us to believe he was wealthy," Mr. Laurent said. "So it seemed like he just wanted to get to Bouvet like the rest of us."

In the *Counting Countries* podcast interview more than a year after the journey, Baekeland said he planned to return to Bouvet "by his own means."

"The schedule of the cruise company was quite tight," he recalled. "If we had stayed one more day, maybe we could have landed."

Mitsidis, in his self-published account of the Baekeland affair, *The Curious Case of William Baekeland*, asserted that William's pledge to "tame" Bouvet vaulted him into extreme travel legend status. "Through his name, his power, his fortune, he had just reached a position much closer to the deities."

CHAPTER 3

◇◇◇◇◇◇◇◇

A Positive Addiction

Man wants to wander, and he must do so or he shall die.

—SIR RICHARD BURTON

Thirty-some-odd years ago, Don Parrish decided to visit all fifty U.S. states. Completing that feat only stoked his appetite for more, so he set out to apply the same concept on a global basis, visiting every region of every country. He says he's a homebody despite the fact that he has visited all fifty U.S. states, thirty-two Chinese provinces, twenty-eight states in India, eighty-three Russian oblasts, twenty-seven regions of France, sixteen German Länder, and so on. (And these political subdivisions aren't static, so when a new region is created, Parrish goes back to check it off his list. Oh no, South Sudan is now a country? Gotta go back!)

Parrish is recognized as one of the world's most traveled persons by all of the leading country-collecting clubs. His goal is to go everywhere on the planet, and he's been closing in on completing the MTP travel list in recent years. Most of the places left on his to-do list are obscure, remote islands with no regular ferry service or spots that governments have declared off-limits to travelers.

Parrish is a trim, robust man in his seventies with neatly parted grey hair, pale blue eyes, and a bushy, lumberjack beard. He's a retired telecommunications engineer who looks like he's ready to go back to work at any moment. He wears a Fitbit device to track how many steps he walks each day and keeps a favorite pen tucked in his shirt pocket. His travel obsession started in the summer of 1965 when, as a college student from Texas, he worked as an unskilled laborer in a metal factory in Hanau, West Germany, as part of an exchange program. This formative experience gave him a taste for travel that has only intensified over the years. Travel, he believes, is a pursuit of knowledge, and each trip leads to the next one.

Don Parrish ©Dave Seminara

For hyper-organized Parrish, travel isn't just a pastime or a hobby. He prepares laminated itineraries for each journey, detailing his schedule and goals for the trip. And he has recently begun to record and document every passport stamp he has accrued so he knows exactly when he entered and exited every country he has traveled to over the years. He calls this a "personal travel archaeology" project, and says the point isn't to prove that he's the most traveled person but rather just for his own record-keeping.

"I like to be able to look back and see that on July 7, 1996, on trip number fifty-four [he also assigns each of his trips a number], I was in a particular place," he explained.

I met Parrish for the first time in a small park near his home in Downers Grove, a suburb of Chicago. He arrived early and had a black briefcase with some of his laminated trip itineraries and books detailing all his passport stamps. We had a lot to talk about but had a hard time agreeing on how to proceed. Parrish is a methodical, analytical thinker and he quickly grew frustrated when I would interrupt one of his stories to ask a question.

"We'll get to that," he'd say.

Parrish travels with his own pillow and has no souvenirs in his home—he doesn't like to waste money, and the place isn't big enough.

"Some people spend their money on nice clothes and fancy cars," he said. "I spend my money on travel."

The only evidence of his travels inside his home is a map of the world in a hallway. But, no, there are no pins to indicate where he's been.

"There would be pins everywhere," he explained.

Most pleasure trips are for a finite period of time to specific destinations. The journey is supposed to provide a solution—it could be anything from satisfying curiosity about a place or needing a break from routine to seeing a specific sight, finding a partner, or any other purpose.

But for those inflicted with intensive wanderlust, these trips provide a powerful sense of momentum. Visit Thailand and you'll meet travelers who swear that Laos is more authentic. Go to Laos and others will insist that you haven't seen a thing until you've been to Cambodia. The next thing you know, you've quit your job and are living out of a suitcase.

Once you're hooked on travel, you can never really feel sated because it's not really a small world after all. It's immense, and pursuing the bits you haven't seen can evolve into an obsession.

The word "wanderlust" comes from the German verb "*wander*"—"to hike." Wanderlust is literally a desire to hike, but Daniel Garrison Brinton, a surgeon who spent a year traveling after medical school in the 1850s, hit on the deeper meaning of the term in his 1902 book with the not-so-sexy title *The Basis of Social Relations*. (Today this book might be called *The Six-Hour Blowjob*, or something on these lines.) He described wanderlust as an "inexplicable" force, "fraught with consequences to world-history." "This wanderlust arises as an emotional epidemic, not by a process of reasoning," he wrote.

Maurice Farber, a longtime professor of psychology at the University of Connecticut who died in 2009, neatly summarized how compulsive travel can become a hamster wheel, where we keep moving without understanding why, in his oft-cited paper,

"Some Hypotheses on the Psychology of Travel," half a century later, in 1954.

"Travel is, for some, a genuine compulsive symptom in the sense that it reflects persistent and powerful unconscious strivings," he wrote.

Indeed, travel is as addictive as sugar, cigarettes, or any drug. Good trips, bad trips, mediocre trips—in some ways, it hardly matters when you just need your next fix. And wanderlust can indeed be an emotional epidemic, as Garrison Brinton suggested more than a century ago. I avoid using the term "travel bug" because a "bug" is a minor affliction that disappears quickly. No, wanderlust is indeed more like an epidemic—something powerful that isn't easy to shake or disregard. A force of nature.

We know a lot about compulsive and neurotic behaviors—hoarding, phobias, and addictions to gambling, drugs, sex, porn, and food—but very little has been written about compulsive wandering. Many travelers freely admit that they are "addicted" to travel, but these admissions are made in a light-hearted context: almost no one thinks of travel as a potentially serious problem because—let's face it—for most of us, travel is fun.

Can travel be a bona fide addiction? You won't find travel addicts convulsing on the floor in a cold sweat like a heroin addict going through withdrawal. And there are no twelve-step programs, halfway houses, or methadone clinics for the afflicted. But compulsive travelers can become dependent on travel to achieve a high they can't find anywhere else. And that dependence makes it difficult for us to come home.

Anyone—even the president of the United States of America—can feel a little lost at the end of a long journey. After two terms as

U.S. president, Ulysses S. Grant left the White House on uncertain financial footing, but, rather than try to cash in on his notoriety, he elected to indulge his wanderlust, taking a two-year-and-four-month-long journey around the world.

Biographer Ron Chernow said that Grant displayed "inexhaustible curiosity about the daily habits of ordinary people, seeking out obscure nooks of cities where he could watch them incognito." His wife, Julia Grant, devoted a third of her memoir to describing the trip.

They traveled with their sons for part of the journey and were nomads during this time period, with no fixed abode in the U.S. As they sailed back to San Francisco from Japan in September 1879, Grant, according to Chernow, "returned home with some trepidation, even a creeping sense of dread, unsure of how he would make a living or even where he would live." Writing to his friend and former secretary of state, Elihu Washburne, Grant said, "I have no home but must establish one after I get back. I do not know where."

Grant later told reporters that he was homesick a year into his journey but had gotten used to the vagabonding lifestyle and rather liked it.

"A year and a half ago, I was thoroughly homesick, but the variation of scene and the kindness which I have met with have almost done away with that feeling."

The Grants ended up living nomadically for four years. The former president thought he couldn't afford to live in a city but he found Galena, Illinois, where he grew up, too depressing. They landed on their feet, settling in New York City in an apartment on East Sixty-Sixth Street, across from Central Park, thanks to a $100,000 gift from wealthy benefactors. Sadly, health problems prevented him from repeating his world tour and he died of throat cancer in 1885.

❖　❖　❖

The natural inclination for the obsessed traveler is to exterminate that post-travel depression by planning a new trip. The problem is that few of us have the luxury of traveling wherever and whenever we damn well feel like it. Work and family commitments, not to mention limited finances, can keep us grounded. And even if you try to structure a career path to accommodate a travel addiction, there are obstacles to overcome.

Ruth Engs, a professor of public health at Indiana University, told me that any activity or behavior can turn into an addiction. "Some activities [like travel] are 'positive addictions' but they can disrupt personal, family, work, financial stability, and other life commitments and can be considered an addictive behavior," she says.

Dr. Joseph Troiani, a professor of psychology at Adler University, echoed that assertion, telling me that travel can turn into a compulsive behavior for people who are looking to escape reality or use it as an avoidance strategy.

"It can be a way to delay or completely avoid doing things we don't want to do," he says. "It's easy to get hooked on travel because it stimulates the pleasure centers in the brain."

Even if there's general agreement that just about any behavior can turn into an addiction, I wanted to find a therapist accustomed to treating much nastier addictions—drugs, sex, porn, gambling— to see if they would take a self-diagnosed travel addiction seriously.

I found Pete Pennington, a Bend, Oregon-based psychotherapist with a master's degree in clinical mental health counseling, specializing in gambling and other addictions, on the website of the magazine *Psychology Today*. A fit guy with fine straw-colored hair whom I took to be around my age—forty-five—Pennington ushered me inside a fluorescently lit office adorned with a bike, an aquarium, and a dry-erase board still filled with notes from his previous client, a gambling addict who was smiling as she exited the building. (Had she just won the lottery?)

"I just finished a really intense session, so I'm a little wiped out," Pennington said, taking a photo of his notes from the dry-erase board.

I felt a bit uneasy introducing the topic of travel addiction after he had just treated someone with what most would consider a much more serious and dangerous condition. I was like the guy waiting in line at the police station to flag a jaywalker behind someone reporting a murder. But Pennington set me at ease by establishing early on that he too was a traveler. In 2009, he left his job as a wilderness therapist to take a ten-month trip to India, Nepal, Southeast Asia, and a host of other places. But although he enjoyed the trip, travel never evolved into an addiction.

He loved some of the places he visited (Thailand) but was ambivalent or down on others (Egypt). Coming home wasn't an ordeal.

"There is no such thing as a positive addiction," he said, disagreeing with what I'd heard from Ruth Engs. "An addiction is when the negative consequences of a behavior outweigh the positive ones."

Pennington said that travel helped him bring the same sense of curiosity he had while in an exotic place back home.

"When I was sitting in traffic in Kathmandu, I never felt bored because there was always something interesting to look at," he said. "I try to be the same way here in Bend. I look around. I try to be observant rather than spacing out."

I told Pennington a bit about my life as a traveler and about some of the fellow travel addicts I've met. But he was undecided on the question of whether travel could be a legitimate addiction. In more than ten years of treating clients, he'd worked with bipolar types, depressives, hoarders, people with eating and anxiety disorders, and those with addictions to gambling, sex, porn, alcohol, and drugs. But he had never treated anyone with a travel addiction.

"Travel is a complex experience," he said, stroking a few days of beard growth on his chin. "People are usually addicted to really simple things. I'm not saying travel addiction doesn't exist but I just don't know. My instinct is that it's not the travel that's someone's problem but rather some other underlying issue in their life that's troubling them."

Since Pennington specializes in gambling addiction, I asked him if most of the gamblers he treats acknowledge their addiction.

"Most of them don't because addictions disrupt our perception of reality," he said. "I show them all the statistics about how people who gamble or play the lottery don't win but it means nothing to them. They're all convinced that they'll win if they keep playing."

Pennington might not see it, but I see parallels between gambling and compulsive traveling. Both pursuits can turn into costly obsessions that can impact careers, relationships, and pocketbooks. And while the gambler thinks if he just keeps rolling the dice, eventually he'll strike it big, at least some travelers believe that if they keep moving, they'll find Shangri-la, enlightenment or the person who will change their life.

In early 2019, William wrote me a letter from India after I informed him that I was writing a book. "Addiction specialists would indeed be a good reference point," he said. But William strongly denied that he was an addict:

> I deny the allegation of being a travel addict. I am someone who likes to travel, absolutely. For those who know me well, and I have discussed this to varying extents with some others within the 'travel community' (their faux-term, not mine), travel is not my primary obsession in this life, it is one of my interests which provides a real world basis of understanding for various other things. My own personal travels are highly focused on specific subjects and are designed in a systematic method… In short, this comprises of a division of the world within a period of approximately 48 months. This is not continuous, of course, I am not interested in being away for so long and to travel so intensively for such a period of time. It is not really for me to say if this is addictive behaviour, but I don't believe it is. I consider it to be highly rationalised (for me) and focused – the opposite of addiction.

❖ ❖ ❖

Wanderlust starts with curiosity. Not everyone needs to travel to satisfy curiosity. I had an uncle who was a very learned guy with a high degree of intellectual curiosity. But he was able to satisfy his curiosity by reading books rather than going on trips. Is curiosity an inherited trait? If not, what is its underlying cause?

George Loewenstein, a professor of economics and psychology at Carnegie Mellon University, published what is still probably the definitive review and reinterpretation of the psychology of curiosity in 1994. Lowenstein called curiosity a "critical motive that influences behavior in both positive and negative ways at all stages of the life cycle." Researchers have established a strong link between curiosity and exploratory behavior, and Loewenstein calls curiosity a "natural human tendency to make sense of the world."

Curiosity was a major impetus behind scientific discovery and has served to inspire and stimulate creative types throughout history. But on the downside, it is also associated with behavior disorders one can find as search categories on porn sites, such as voyeurism, and is often blamed for risky behaviors such as drug and alcohol use, early sexual experimentation, and certain types of crime such as arson.

Loewenstein calls curiosity a "form of cognitively induced deprivation that results from the perception of a gap in one's knowledge." The more knowledge one gains in a field, the more the curious person will focus on what they don't know. Curiosity increases with knowledge and as people focus on one area, they can become obsessed with it and realize their shortcomings. The more you travel, the more aware you are of the gaps on your travel resume, particularly if you dwell in the company of the world's elite competitive travelers. The quest for mastery and completion, i.e., finishing the travel lists, is a powerful one that can be hard to set aside.

In our modern context, curiosity is viewed as almost universally positive. But it hasn't always been this way. In Greek mythology, Pandora, the first woman created by the gods, succumbed to her curiosity, opening a box (probably a jar) that released all the evils of humanity. Eve ate the forbidden fruit from the tree of knowledge, and in the book of Genesis, Lot's wife was so curious that she couldn't resist turning around to look at the city of Sodom. The poor woman—she wasn't named in the bible, other than "Lot's wife"—was turned into a pillar of salt.

Stephen Greenblatt, a Pulitzer Prize-winning author and professor of the humanities at Harvard, noted in *The New York Times Review of Books* in 1998 that for centuries, "Stoic philosophers and Christian theologians struggled to subdue curiosity as one of the most disruptive, intractable and potentially vicious human traits."

In the twelfth century, a French abbot, St. Bernard of Clairvaux, wrote that curiosity was "the first step of pride…the beginning of all sin." He detailed twelve steps up the mountain of pride, and another twelve steps down in his work *The Steps of Humility and Pride*. Curiosity, he asserted, can be healthy, but it can also be sinful when we take it too far, prying into matters that are not our concern.

Apparently some still believe this. Monsignor Charles Pope, a pastor in the Archdiocese of Washington, D.C., concluded in a 2013 piece on the twelve steps that the mountain of pride begins "in the mind with a lack of sobriety rooted in sinful curiosity and frivolous preoccupation."

St. Augustine referred to curiosity as an "ocular lust." Cicero thought that the story of Odysseus—the hero of Homer's epic poem *The Odyssey*, who spent ten years making his way home after the Trojan War—was a parable about curiosity. Some two thousand years ago he remarked, "It was the passion for learning that kept men rooted to the Siren's rocky shores." And the nineteenth-century German philosopher Ludwig Feuerbach viewed curiosity as invoking "painful feelings of deprivation if not satisfied."

Loewenstein echoed this concern, observing that, "Despite its transience, curiosity can exert a powerful motivational force. Like sexual attraction, curiosity often produces impulsive behavior and attempts at self control…. People who are curious not only desire information but desire it immediately and even seek it out against their better judgment."

Researchers don't agree on why we do this but they have identified multiple types of curiosity. One type, referred to as diversive curiosity, which is a kind of general stimulation seeking, is probably most closely related to novelty seeking and exploratory behavior, but it can also be a garden-variety response to boredom. In 1972, the influential psychologist Jerome Kagan identified four basic human motives—the first, the motive to resolve uncertainty, is synonymous with curiosity. (The others are sensory motives, anger and hostility, and the motive for mastery.)

Loewenstein argued that the key to understanding curiosity seeking "lies in recognizing that the process of satisfying curiosity is itself pleasurable." And the process of satiating one's curiosity can indeed be enormously gratifying. But Loewenstein also acknowledged that while "the satisfaction one obtains from satisfying curiosity will undoubtedly occasionally exceed one's expectations," he believes that those instances are outnumbered by occasions where the result is disappointing.

With respect to travel, it's a thrill to wonder what Zambia is like. But when we step off the plane, we may or may not be impressed. Either way, for those of us who are obsessed with exploration, it won't stop us from booking that next trip. We're junkies in need of a fix. For ordinary travelers, fixes are a few clicks of the mouse away. But for the extreme traveler seeking to get to the world's most challenging destinations, you need a good dealer—someone like William—to get the right fix.

CHAPTER 4

◇◇◇◇◇◇◇◇

Drug Dealer

*The end for every drug dealer is the cemetery or
the jail cell. No drug dealer has ever retired.*

—Pablo Escobar

David Langan is a philatelist. The fifty-seven-year-old Irishman
has a successful furniture business in Dublin, and he has the
freedom and passion to pursue his goal of sending himself a
postcard from every geographic entity on the planet that issues
stamps. The only countries where he was unable to do this were
South Sudan and Somalia, which have no functioning postal service. Guatemala's postal service is also dysfunctional—at least for
the public—but Langan is so committed to his global stamp-col-
lecting pursuit that he found a government contact who was able
to help him get the Guatemalan postmark he needed. In North

Korea, the postal service was functional, he says, but when he tried to send a postcard with a photo of the Dear Leader, he was told it was impossible because the postmark would go on the exulted leader's head.

"If the country is dodgy, I'll send postcards from multiple locations," he says. "I think I've only had eleven postcards that haven't come back in all these years."

Langan has traveled just about everywhere, and has nine books full of postcards he has sent himself from every corner of the planet. But there are still some places he needs to visit. The Donetsk region of Ukraine, which now issues its own stamps, is a target, as is Niuafo'ou, an obscure island in Tonga that has only about 650 inhabitants. Also called Tin Can Island, it has its own stamps to recognize its past, when mail was delivered and picked up by strong swimmers who would retrieve packages sealed in biscuit tins and thrown overboard from passing ships.

Langan travels systematically and appreciates travel lists because they give him a way to organize his travel goals. But he also thinks that some of the top travelers become preoccupied with their rankings and lose perspective.

"It's like dealing with drugs," he says. "Once you get it in your system, you *have* to have it. When you're on a trip, it's like a high, and you do whatever you have to do to get that."

Though he says he isn't concerned about his rankings in the travel clubs, Langan took pride in being the number-one-ranked Irish traveler in the MTP rankings. Until, that is, sometime after the Bouvet trip in 2013 when he noticed that a young man named William Baekeland with an Irish flag next to his name and an astonishing travel resume had overtaken him for the number-one spot.

"None of it made sense," he recalls. "It wasn't an Irish name and, you know, Ireland is a pretty small place. He claimed to have been to some very remote, obscure places, and if it was real, I think I would have heard of him before, but I hadn't."

Langan also noticed that young Baekeland claimed to have been to Bouvet. But he knew from others that the recent cruise there hadn't landed. The Irishman's curiosity was piqued, so he exchanged emails with William and a few months later, the two met for dinner at Trocadero, a venerable restaurant in a handsome old Georgian building on St. Andrew's Street in the heart of Dublin. Langan had exchanged emails with Harry Mitsidis, who, as the founder of NomadMania/TBT, is a kind of extreme travel ambassador, and Mitsidis had assured him that Baekeland was a legit trust-fund type, with huge resources and a massive travel resume.

When Langan entered the restaurant, William, dressed neatly in a blazer and fashionable buttoned-down shirt, was already sitting at the table.

"He came across as very believable," Langan recalls. "With his accent, he could have been on the BBC. He seemed like a gentle, kind of shy type of person. With his demeanor and the way he dressed, it was almost like he was too old for his age."

Their conversation revolved mostly around travel, and William's knowledge of destinations around the world left Langan convinced that the kid was the real deal. He seemed like someone who very well could have been the heir to a great fortune. "I didn't ask him, 'How did you get your money?'" Langan says. "But everything he said seemed to suggest that 'Money isn't an object and I don't need to work.'"

William said he lived at the K Club, a restored Georgian estate that's a luxurious five-star golf and spa resort with a residential community of some eighty-three homes and apartments in County Kildare, about forty minutes outside Dublin.

WILLIAM S. BAEKELAND

822 LADYCASTLE
THE KILDARE COUNTRY CLUB
STRAFFAN
CO. KILDARE
REPUBLIC OF IRELAND

T: +353 1 627 8717
M: +353 872 123 547

WILLIAM@BAEKELAND.CO.UK

It seemed like an odd place for a young man to live alone, Langan thought, but William seemed like a bit of a loner. He said that he managed lands in Scotland, but was vague on the details.

Langan, who is gay, had heard that William was also gay and so he asked him if he might like to check out a gay group in Dublin he's a part of. But Baekeland quickly changed the subject.

Langan later asked him about Tony Baekeland and how he killed his mother. "He said, 'I can't talk about that,' and that was it."

Baekeland ordered spaghetti and had a glass of water and they split the bill. William told Langan that he was a pilot and planned to go everywhere. There was no reason to think he was lying.

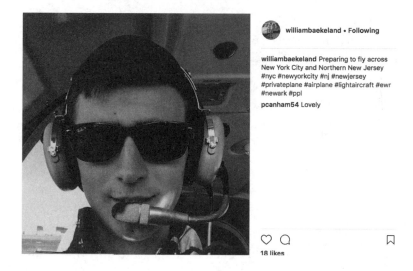

williambaekeland • Following

williambaekeland Preparing to fly across New York City and Northern New Jersey #nyc #newyorkcity #nj #newjersey #privateplane #airplane #lightaircraft #ewr #newark #ppl

pcanham54 Lovely

18 likes

The pair stayed in sporadic touch but William never invited Langan on any of the offbeat trips he was organizing for country collectors. Langan says he didn't need William's help getting to the places he wanted to go anyway. They didn't cross paths again until August 2017 at a NomadMania-organized trip/conference to the Layang-Layang Island Resort in the (disputed) Spratly Island archipelago in the South China Sea.

By this point, William was a Zen master in the world of extreme travel. In a tight-knit community where word traveled fast, he had accompanied or arranged trips for some of the world's top-ranked travelers to a host of difficult destinations on the travel lists—places like the Isla de Aves, a tiny island off the coast of Venezuela, the war-torn Central African Republic, and Marion Island, a generally off-limits subantarctic island that's nine days by treacherous seas from Cape Town.

Though he didn't go on this trip, William's ingenuity was on full display in planning it. He was somehow able to determine that South African officials would be traveling to the island's research station to service a nitrogen generator that's used to create weather bulletins.

Baekeland was able to finagle four travelers, including Babis Bizas—a Greek man who also has a claim to the "world's most traveled man" title—onto the list of engineers cleared to visit the island.

"How did he do it? I don't know," Bizas says. "We spent 209 hours on the boat. We ate humble food from cans like animals. There was no service. It was the worst trip I have ever done. But we wanted to be there and were happy for that. It changed my life and my travel concept. After this, I knew I could get to the world's most remote islands."

And even a daring, some would say foolish, failed expedition to Scarborough Shoal, a disputed territory in the South China Sea where their boat was turned around by the Chinese Navy, seemed to only enhance his reputation as a bold adventurer who was breaking open previously closed destinations.

Baekeland also gained credibility by taking part in other trips with country collectors he didn't organize, such as expeditions to Clipperton Island, an uninhabited French atoll in the Pacific, the Ross Sea in Antarctica, and an extreme traveler conference organized by Kolja Spöri, a man whom many consider the dean of extreme travel, in Mogadishu, Somalia. Fellow travelers in the Somali capital noticed that he was one of only two participants who booked a business-class ticket on the flight there, and he was the only one who had somehow pre-booked a room on the highest floor of the hotel, the Jazeera Palace, with extra security, including reinforced doors plus an armed guard near the elevator.

Langan says that at the Layang-Layang Resort, William held court on a poolside recliner, surrounded by admirers.

"People flocked to him," Langan recalls. "The trips are like drugs for these people, and it was like sitting down with the drug dealer who's telling you where he can take you. They would throw out places they wanted to go, like these little rocks and atolls, and he'd say 'Oh yes, I can bring you there.' They were like kids in a toy shop."

William on Clipperton Island ©Dominique Laurent

Harry Mitsidis described the main "task" of this particular NomadMania conference as to "consider and reconsider NomadMania's division of the world into 1281 regions." The vigorous debate and the subsequent voting reveal how seriously extreme travelers take these matters. Mitsidis reported in his book, *The Curious Case of William Baekeland,* that the travelers considered whether Russia's Wrangel Island should be considered its own point, if Lesotho merited a second region, and if Ireland should have three rather than four regions, among other hotly contested issues.

William, the only traveler in the group who never appeared bare-chested or in a swimsuit, didn't act like a salesman, Langan says. He was accepted as a member of the club, a guy who was letting them in on his semi-secret expeditions.

"It suited the way these people act; it was like, 'Shhhh, I've only got six spots on this trip,'" Langan says. "His demeanor was perfect for them. To them, it's a competition—'I've been there but you haven't been.' It was exclusive."

CHAPTER 5
◇◇◇◇◇◇◇◇

Mad Travelers

All that is gold does not glitter,
not all those who wander are lost.

—J. R. R. TOLKIEN

Jean-Albert Dadas was a French laborer who left work in Bordeaux one day in 1885 and proceeded to wander around the world off and on for more than a year, often forgetting who he was. He eventually resurfaced in a French mental hospital, where he could recall details of what his doctors called his "obsessive and uncontrollable journeys" to Moscow, North Africa, and Istanbul only when hypnotized. They diagnosed Dadas as a "pathological" traveler and referred to him in a clinical report as a kind of "new wandering Jew," even though he was not Jewish. Other doctors categorized his traveling episodes as "fugues" and classified Dadas with a new diagnosis:

dromomania, which they described as a "compulsive drive toward taking flight."

The case touched off a "mad traveler" hysteria in Europe, documented in Ian Hacking's book *Mad Travelers: Reflections on the Reality of Transient Mental Illnesses*, where hundreds of people— many of them probably suffering from head injuries, epilepsy, or other ailments—were diagnosed with this compulsive wandering disorder. Hacking concludes that the fugues documented around Europe at this time reflected the "darker side of travel" that existed somewhere between tourism and vagrancy.

The "mad traveler" hysteria died out in 1909, after a conference in Nantes in which medical professionals developed a host of new diagnoses to replace fugue. The roving mystery novelist Agatha Christie was said to have lapsed into an eleven-day-long fugue state in 1926, and the Walter White character in the TV show *Breaking Bad* famously claimed to have lapsed into a fugue state to cover up his drug dealing. But dromomania diagnoses have been rare in recent decades. In fact, fugue isn't considered a central nervous system disorder anymore but rather an incident that can occur if you have a number of other ailments.

It's worth noting that we still don't understand fugue states very well because most of the legions of homeless people we see wandering the streets with shopping carts or backpacks aren't treated. Do they have a compulsion to wander, are they mentally ill, or are they simply down on their luck?

And what about people who roam because they've been spurned by their families or the wider society, for one reason or another? Consider an article titled "Girl Blames Wanderlust" from the June 13, 1910, edition of the *New York Times*. The story describes a young lady named Olive Parker, the daughter of an orchestra leader who was taken to a Manhattan hospital after being found wandering the streets in boy's clothing. The article asserted that she was in the habit of wandering, sometimes for months at a time, always in boy's clothing. "Every now and then, she gets what her friends describe as 'wanderlust' and leaves home for a while," wrote the author. Who knows whether young Olive had wanderlust or a gender identity issue, but it's easy to see how one could feed into the other.

Compulsive travelers tend to be what psychologists call novelty seekers. We get bored easily and seek out stimuli—new people, new places, new relationships, new flavors of puppy chow—it can be any novel experience. On one level, this behavior is triggered by dopamine, a hormone that plays a number of important roles in the human brain. Dopamine functions as a neurotransmitter, associated with processing rewards, new stimuli, movement, cognition, and sociability.

Rewards like travel increase the level of dopamine in the brain. Researchers have found that novelty seekers have higher levels of a specific type of receptor (D4) for dopamine, which is the neurotransmitter involved with reward processing. Novelty seekers have less of other dopamine receptors that put the brakes on thrill-seeking behavior. Our dopaminergic differences (say that five times fast) help explain why some are eager to explore new places while others focus on the dangers of doing so, preferring to park their keisters at home.

Captain James Cook is one of history's best examples of a person who wasn't afraid to explore new places—even at tremendous personal risk and hardship. He grew up poor, the son of a farm laborer, and became one of the world's greatest navigators. Cook could have dined out for life after his first voyage across the Pacific on the *HMS Endeavour*. Instead, and despite the fact that he was a family man in his forties with six children, he made two more epic journeys of discovery in the Pacific, across mostly uncharted waters, before being stabbed to death on a beach in Hawaii at fifty.

According to Tony Horwitz's *Blue Latitudes: Boldly Going Where Captain Cook Has Gone Before,* Cook recorded a sense of discovery in stumbling across the Great Barrier Reef on the first Pacific journey that he was never able to duplicate.

"The farther he went, the less pleasure exploration seemed to give him," Horwitz wrote. "Toward the end, he would rail against everything: his indefatigable sailors, his superiors, even the wind."

Novelty seeking, or "neophilia," has long been associated with trouble. Researchers have linked it to attention deficit hyperactivity disorder (ADHD), compulsive behaviors, and even criminal tendencies. But in her book *New: Understanding Our Need for Novelty and Change*, Winifred Gallagher asserts that neophilia has also been a critical human survival skill.

Gallagher contends that as a nation of immigrants, the United States is the most neophilic society in history. She argues that technology is turning many of us, especially young people, into a nation of easily bored novelty seekers. Neophilia may help us explore and create, the author maintains, but it also fuels "chronic restlessness and distraction."

Perhaps so, but nearly a century ago the poet and essayist Ralph Waldo Emerson said that the "rage of travelling is a symptom of a deeper unsoundness affecting the whole intellectual action. The intellect is vagabond, and our system of education fosters restlessness. Our minds travel when our bodies are forced to stay at home."

Gallagher asserts that 10–15 percent of us are neophobes who are biased toward routine and playing it safe, another 10–15 percent of the population are neophiliacs who crave novelty, risk, and change, and the remaining 70–80 percent are moderate neophiles who fall somewhere in between.

A significant problem for the neophiliacs among us, Gallagher says, is the adaption process, where we become accustomed to the novel experience and no longer derive enjoyment from it. (Like Captain Cook, who wrote in his journal, "Ambition leads me not only farther than any other man has been before me, but as far as I think it possible for man to go.") A pause in the behavior can slow down the adaptation process, as can things that are counterintuitive or otherwise difficult for our brains to easily categorize or process.

Gallagher's research on adaption resonated with me because though I have spent much of my life craving travel opportunities, I've also come to the depressing realization that on long trips I can't sustain the high I get from discovering new places. After the initial burst of excitement that accompanies breaking out of my home life routine upon arrival in a new place, I eventually grow accustomed to the traveling lifestyle. I still enjoy it, but the rush dissolves as the adaptation process sets in.

Perhaps I could reduce my novelty-seeking tendencies? Most experts argue that such an effort would be futile. Washington University psychiatrist C. Robert Cloninger has identified novelty seeking as one of four basic "temperaments." The other three are harm avoidance (aversion to risk), reward dependence (being sensitive to social situations and reinforcement), and persistence. Cloninger concluded that these temperaments are mostly inherited—some of us are hardwired to embrace the new, others to avoid it.

In a piece on neophiliacs for *Psychology Today*, Dr. Susan Krauss Whitbourne concluded that novelty seeking was essentially a "mixed bag."

"To get the most benefit from novelty seeking, it's important to keep the balance in mind between sameness and change," she said. "New may be better than old, but not at the cost to your mental health."

Gallagher counsels neophiliacs to "stop using curiosity like a floodlight and start focusing it like a laser on the new things that promise long-term benefits…taking time to re- identify your priorities and the subjects worth an investment of your finite interest is a productive exercise in itself." Develop a critical attitude, Gallagher says, about the value of novelty and change.

That sounds reasonable enough, but how does one control that novelty-seeking impulse? How does a compulsive traveler learn to tolerate or even enjoy routine? Science writer Sharon Begley concludes in her book *Can't Just Stop: An Investigation of Compulsions* that compulsions are responses to anxiety. "Compulsions come from a need so desperate, burning and tortured it makes us feel like a vessel filled with steam, saturating us with a hot urgency that demands relief," she writes.

Our novelty-seeking impulses are said to drop in half between the ages of twenty and sixty. This means that just as we acquire the time to wander during retirement, our desire to do so wanes. And yet, many of the world's top travelers are over sixty, so this is far from a golden rule.

Every addiction typically involves the inability to stop the behavior. Most obsessive travelers, myself included, would say that they could stop traveling anytime. But pulling the plug can be a bit like allowing a pit bull to chow on the cushiony part of your ass.

Maurizio Giuliano is an Italian traveler of forty-odd years who thinks that travel is a genetic addiction. He made it into *The Guinness Book of World Records* at twenty-eight, as the youngest man to visit every sovereign nation. Giuliano knew he needed to find a "wanderlust compliant" occupation, so he gravitated toward international development.

Maurizio Giuliano

When I interviewed him via Skype, he was working in a remote corner of the Democratic Republic of Congo while his Afghan wife and two children lived in Switzerland. He gets about three months off each year, but spends some of that time satisfying his wanderlust in remote corners of the planet.

"It's an addiction, but you can find coping mechanisms to deal with it," he says.

Jean Béliveau, a fifty-nine-year-old Montreal native, spent eleven years walking around the world. On his forty-fifth birthday, he crossed Montreal's Jacques Cartier Bridge—where he originally dreamed up the idea of escaping his life as a neon sign salesman nine months before—and kept going for 75,554 kilometers. He wore out fifty-four pairs of shoes as he walked through sixty-four countries.

When he returned home in 2011, he told his longtime partner, Luce, that his traveling days were over. But three years after I first interviewed Jean, he sent me an email detailing a new plan to walk across Colombia and the impenetrable Darién Gap that separates Central and South America, two spots that he missed on his walk around the world. "I felt like a lion in a cage being at home all this time," he said.

Why do travelers like me, Jean, Maurizio and many others find the allure of the road irresistible? Addiction expert Gabor Maté told author Johann Hari in his book, *Chasing the Scream: The First and Last Days of the War on Drugs*, that addiction usually involves a combination of a potentially addictive behavior or substance and a "susceptible" person.

Bruce K. Alexander, a professor at Simon Fraser University in British Columbia, tells Hari that addictive behavior is increasingly common because of social dislocation. "Our hyper- individualistic, frantic, crisis-ridden society makes most people feel socially or culturally isolated. Chronic isolation causes people to look for relief. They find temporary relief in addiction."

In other words, we're social animals living in a largely antisocial age of social media, texting, and other forms of faux social interactions that are about as fulfilling as an afternoon spent watching the Home Shopping Network.

But men have been compelled to wander since long before the smartphone was invented.

And so the question endures—how does a casual traveler become a compulsive one?

CHAPTER 6

◇◇◇◇◇◇◇◇

Country Collecting

Collecting seems to bring out that primi-
tive instinct for the hunt in some of its dev-
otees, who stalk their prey with skill.

—ALICIA CRAIG FAXON

The country-collecting avocation dates to 1954, when Bert Hemphill, the owner of a travel agency that pioneered round-the-world trips, and his tour director, Russell Davidson, founded the Travelers' Century Club (TCC) in Los Angeles. By 1960 they had forty-three members who were able to prove that they had traveled to a hundred or more countries. Unlike MTP and NomadMania, TCC has never established formal rankings, but a 1974 profile in the *New York Times* asserted that Hemphill—who had by that point made thirty-eight trips around the world, or so he claimed—was the group's most traveled member.

The *Times* reported, "Even in today's jet age, the club has had trouble soaring over the 300 member mark." In order to boost membership, TCC welcomed anyone who visited at least a hundred places, rather than a hundred countries, on what was then a list of 263 destinations. In 1974, the United Nations had only 138 member countries; today there are 193. And there are now more than 1,400 TCC members and 325 places on the list. Anyone who says they've been to a hundred countries can join, and members are honored when they reach different levels on the TCC list: 150 (Silver), 200 (Gold), 250 (Platinum), and 300 (Diamond).

No one knows for sure how many travelers have visited every UN country but country collectors believe the figure is somewhere near two hundred. The *Counting Countries* podcast intro asserts that there are more people who have traveled to outer space than have made it to all 193 countries.

The Guinness Book of World Records recognized John Clouse in 1995 as the world's most traveled man. Ten years later, Charles Veley founded MTP after approaching Guinness in the hopes of laying claim to the most traveled title. Veley is a pioneering figure in the world of country collecting and his life story is a great one. He went to Harvard on an ROTC scholarship but was dismissed from the air force due to a vision problem. He went on to found a tech company that went public. Flush with money—at one point he was worth $166 million on paper—he quit his job in 2000 and went on a country-collecting rampage, becoming the youngest person, at thirty-seven, to complete the TCC list in 2003. He was in Tasmania one day on one of his round-the-world trips when his company's stock price plummeted, losing 75 percent of its value in one day. Soon he'd need to return to work as his fortune dwindled.

In a 2019 interview on the *Counting Countries* podcast, Veley was candid in looking back at his frenetic travels, in which he took more than three hundred flights in some years. "It wasn't really enjoyable travel at all," he said. "It was a lot of flights and not much sightseeing. Today I'd say it was superficial travel. It wasn't worth it."

Veley founded MTP because he felt he could improve on the TCC list and unlike TCC he established traveler rankings. And he's serious about travel integrity—he said on the *Counting Countries* podcast that he once lost a laptop that contained all the proof that he'd been to a couple dozen places on his list and he revisited all those places to ensure he had proof in case anyone ever asked. "That was my personal standard," he said.

Veley's 874-place club gave extreme travelers new goals and ways to measure themselves against each other. (He was eventually eclipsed in his own club rankings by Bob Bonifas and Don Parrish as he went back to work after years spent mostly on the road, but made a comeback and is now number one again.) In 2011, Mitsidis founded TBT (which he later renamed NomadMania), an online club with a 1,281-place list that rewards (ranked) travelers who have visited every region of every country.

Jorge Sánchez is a reluctant country collector who frequently critiques his fellow extreme travelers. The Spaniard dropped out of school at fourteen and has made his way in life, traveling around the world while intermittently working as a waiter, a dishwasher, a driver, and many other odd jobs. A handsome, lantern-jawed, robustly built man in his early sixties, he has thick hair and olive skin. He could pass for fifty. Sánchez says that he has no real profession and hasn't worked enough to merit a pension. He's been too busy traveling—and has no regrets.

Jorge Sánchez ©Jorge Sánchez

Sánchez has visited every sovereign nation, plus every region in every major country, and scores of obscure islands, like Tristan da Cunha—an impossibly isolated locale that is reached only via a twenty-day round-trip boat journey from South Africa. He has slept under bridges in India, in telephone booths in China, up a tree in Brazil, inside a morgue in Liechtenstein, in prisons in Colombia, Paraguay, Georgia, and Afghanistan—where he was mistaken for a spy—and as a pilgrim in houses of worship representing every major world religion.

His mission is to travel to every place on Earth, and, according to NomadMania/TBT—which rates him the third most widely traveled person on the planet—he has visited 1163 of 1281 places on TBT's travel to-do list. Almost all the places missing from his travel resume are hard-to-get-to islands that few aside from frenzied travel zealots have heard of. They include geographic oddities like Franz Josef Land, a group of 191 frigid, uninhabited islands near the North Pole; Marie Byrd Land, a chunk of West Antarctica so remote that no nation has even claimed it; and Juan de Nova Island, a 1.7-square-mile tropical island between Mozambique and Madagascar that was named after a Spanish admiral who stumbled across the place in 1501.

For obsessive club travelers, one's travel resume can be quantified based on the number of countries, territories, autonomous regions, enclaves, geographically separated island groups, and major states and provinces they have visited. Extreme travelers want to go "everywhere," but they do not agree on what that term means.

The very top travelers have virtually nothing but dangerous or off-limits places left to visit. Hitting these spots often requires both luck and ingenuity. Bob Bonifas found a way to visit Guantanamo because he knew someone who knew someone who was stationed there and could give him the required official invite. He also found a way to get to the officially off-limits Gaza Strip through a Pole with a UN connection who got them there in exchange for a $5,000 donation to an eye clinic in Gaza.

Other hotspots can be even more difficult to reach and are potentially dangerous upon arrival. MTP has India's Andaman Islands on its list; Don Parrish and Bob Bonifas visited in 2010. Eight years later, John Allen Chau, a twenty-six-year-old American traveler and missionary, was murdered on an off-limits island (North Sentinel) in the Andaman and Nicobar Island chain by the Sentinelese, a pre-Neolithic tribe of perhaps a couple hundred who have lived without contact from the outside world for centuries and are protected by the Indian government.

Chau paid some local fisherman $354 to take him to the island and, on his first attempt, a teenager shot an arrow at him which pierced his waterproof Bible. He returned the next day and the fishermen saw his body being dragged and buried in the sand. Five fishermen, a guide, and a friend of Chau's were arrested for taking him there, but the tribe members who killed him apparently won't face charges.

Two fishermen who strayed onto the island were killed in 2006. A week after their deaths, their bodies were impaled on bamboo stakes facing out to sea as a warning to anyone else considering stopping by their island.

Media coverage of the event and reader comments online leaned heavily toward the idea that Chau deserved to die. Chau's motivation—converting the tribe to Christianity—was different than that of the typical country collector. But his demise illustrates the difficulty competitive travelers face in getting to the ends of the earth. And the reality is that if they run into trouble in a place they're not supposed to be, they're unlikely to receive much sympathy.

For his part, Jorge Sánchez says he won't complete any of the TCC, MTP, or TBT destination lists because he thinks it's immoral to spend a large sum of money to visit uninhabited islands where he feels there is nothing to learn.

At one point, his profile on the MTP site accused other "narcissistic" club members of "shamelessly" exaggerating their travel numbers to inflate their egos. Such drama can be part of this subculture.

Most of the world's elite travelers know each other. They cross paths online and in remote places like Grozny, Chechnya, Mogadishu, Somalia, and Liberland (a micro-nation in the Danube), and Baghdad and Iraq, where they convened for World Extreme Travel Conferences in 2014, 2016, 2017, and 2018. And they often pool resources to charter boats to islands with no ferry services. But it *is* competitive.

Frank Wigand Grosse-Oetringhaus, a retired Siemens executive who was on the 2015 Bouvet trip, has taken the club rankings to another level by creating a master ranking of travelers using their respective ranks in nine different clubs. According to his calculations, which he says are focused on quality travel, he is the world's best-traveled person.

Frank and Teo

Grosse-Oetringhaus, now in his late seventies, retired in 2006 and began to travel "systematically." He resolved to visit every country in the world and came up with a list of five thousand world highlights that he set out to see in a decade. Traveling with his partner, Murallon Teo, a Filipino physician, they moved out of their home in Berlin in 2006, put all their belongings in storage, and lived the life of nomads for more than ten years. They completed their country-collecting quest and visited about 4,700 of the 5,000 highlights on their list by 2016.

Grosse-Oetringhaus once told fellow extreme travelers that he at one point had what he considered the world's best disco, on a square-meter basis, installed in his home in 1970. He details why he believes he's the best-traveled person in the world on his web page. In one post, he poses the question, "If you claim to be #1[,] are you a narcissist?" He continues:

> For athletes it is normal to go for the No. 1. For traveling it is unusual. But if traveling becomes an essential part of your life it is understandable. It is fulfilling to measure your achievements. Especially if you go for a somewhat vague objective like "to see the whole world". I have developed a huge database for only one purpose: To measure if I have achieved my goal [of] seeing the whole world. This was the core idea of my 5000 highlights list.
>
> The problem starts if you state: "I am the best"—the danger of becoming a narcissist, an extremely egocentric person who lives in his own world. But if you try to be objective and ground your claim on widely acknowledged criteria you are not a narcissist, you like competition and you measure achievements. Nothing is wrong with that.

It's easy to see why he felt the need to defend his claim. The notion of travel as a competitive sport may seem peculiar to some, perhaps an example of wanderlust gone wild. But MTP ranks more than sixteen thousand competitive travelers, TBT/NomadMania has more than ten thousand ranked travelers, and TCC has thousands of members in more than twenty chapters around the world. The competition is an intense version of something most travelers want to do: share their travel experiences. It's why we decorate our homes with travel souvenirs, share war stories, and subject our social media followers to more trip photos than they'd like. Where we've been is part of who we are, or at least the image we want to project.

Competitive travelers take the look-at-where-I've-been ethos a step further. Are they motivated by the validation, the status, and the bragging rights that these organizations confer—or by some nobler impulse? When I first heard about the world of country collecting, I suspected that these obsessed voyagers were vain, tick-the-box types who breezed in and out of countries without learning much.

But after getting to know Parrish, Sánchez, and many others, I realized that I had grossly underestimated most of them. The travel lists compel them to visit and learn about places like Navassa—a remote, uninhabited island about halfway between Haiti and Jamaica—that they would otherwise never know about. For them, the world is like a puzzle, waiting to be solved one piece at a time.

The instinct to condemn country collectors stems at least in part from a traveler's impulse to justify what is, let's face it, a mostly indulgent preoccupation. Mike Spencer Brown is a Canadian who spent twenty-three years backpacking around the world and the better part of a chapter condemning country collectors in his book, *The World's Most Travelled Man*. "Their [country collectors] wanderlust is quenched with a poke of their foot over the border and a passport stamp, after which they turn tail and scurry to the next country on their official list," he wrote in 2017.

Spencer Brown never explains to the reader why he's the *most* travelled person relative to others, but he implies that he's a better traveler because he's not counting countries. Yet, oddly enough, he concludes his book with a chapter on—wait for it—his visit to Ireland, his 193rd (and final) country. So apparently he was counting countries too.

None of us have time to see everything. Travelers who dive deep into a handful of countries are no better than those who get a taste of all of them. Travel snobs who want to look down their noses at country collectors should heed an important maxim: there is no wrong way to indulge wanderlust.

❖   ❖   ❖

Elite travelers often pool resources, chartering boats or flights to islands with no ferry or flight services. But for some it is highly competitive, and because trips to the nether regions of the club lists can't be booked on sites like Expedia or through travel agents, William Baekeland was able to emerge as a kind of swami or magic man for the elite country-collecting set.

Grosse-Oetringhaus told me that his yearning for far-off horizons, the Germans call it "*fernweh*," was a healthy pursuit, and not sickness. "I'm not sick," he said. "I'm just a little crazy."

The German traveler was impressed by Baekeland, whom he met on the Bouvet cruise.

"He gave the impression that he had this abundance of money," he said. "Supposedly he had billions, and with a name like his, we never doubted him."

Just like many other top travelers, Frank had heard the stories about this family. "I heard that his mother, Lady Violette, flew a teddy bear first class to New York for her daughter's funeral, and that he rented a helicopter to see the highest lake in Nepal and all these things," he said.

Frank liked William and so, when Baekeland asked for substantial deposits for trips, he paid. Baekeland had promised to take Frank, his partner, and several others on a Southern Ocean circumnavigation round trip from Cape Town—something that had never been done before.

Grosse-Oetringhaus made a €50,000 deposit for what was supposed to be a grand four- month circumnavigation. Artemy Lebedev, a Russian entrepreneur and popular blogger who traveled with William on the *Ortelius*, says he wired a $30,000 deposit to William's Irish bank account. Paul Holland, a retired schoolteacher from Galway, Ireland, who also met William on the Bouvet trip, bumped into him on Campbell Island, an uninhabited subantarctic island well south of New Zealand in February 2017, as they were heading in opposite directions across the Southern Ocean. William reminded him of their circumnavigation discussion from nearly two years before, and a month later Holland used a chunk of money he inherited when his parents died, selling their farm to pay Baekeland a deposit of €28,000.

In each case, there was no contract, just an exchange of emails. Originally scheduled to depart in December 2018, Frank, Artemy, Paul, William, and six other travelers were to pass through perilously rough seas, departing from Ushuaia, at the southern tip of South America, and traveling through a host of obscure places, including the (French-administered) Kerguelen Islands, also appropriately called the Desolation Islands, the Australian Antarctic territory of the Heard and McDonald Islands, which are roughly two-thirds of the way from Madagascar to Antarctica, and, most importantly, Bouvet.

"It [the circumnavigation] would have given me a new level of performance in travel that no one has ever done before," Grosse-Oetringhaus said. "He was one of us, so we believed him."

Why would Frank and the gang willingly pay a huge sum of money to take such a torturous trip that was bound to be hellish? Were they born with the need to explore?

CHAPTER 7

<><><><><><><>

Feeble Inhibitions

To travel is to live.

—Hans Christian Andersen

Bruce Chatwin was a hopelessly restless soul. He believed that humans have the same migratory instincts as animals and was certain that the sedentary lifestyle was toxic for the soul. The late British writer observed that babies in nomadic societies rarely cried because their mothers walked great distances carrying them in slings, and they felt comforted by motion. He maintained that parents in the West unknowingly imitate this behavior by rocking babies to sleep.

"If we need movement from birth, how should we settle down later?" he asked. Chatwin wrote that there are two main inducements to wander—economic or neurotic—and wondered why he had a seemingly irrational, neurotic travel compulsion that left him "restless after a month in a single place, unbearable after two." He planned to write a book addressing this mystery, but according to his biographer, Nicholas Shakespeare, it took him a mere fourteen years to arrive at a thesis.

"When warped in conditions of settlement, [man] found outlets in violence, greed, status-seeking or a mania for the new," Chatwin wrote. The peripatetic British writer wrestled with the project for years and died of AIDS in 1989, before he could produce a viable manuscript. Like many compulsive travelers, he was easily distracted. In the end, the project gave him an excuse to travel with nomadic tribes in Afghanistan, Mauritania, Iran, and West Africa, which was a reward in itself. Sadly his "mania for the new" theory came to fruition when he became too ill to travel, as his penchant for collecting antiques grew from a hobby into a costly compulsion.

Chatwin's abandoned book project is far from the first attempt to make sense of nomadism or some of its root causes, namely curiosity and novelty seeking. In the late nineteenth century, Sigmund Freud asserted that curiosity was a proxy for sexual curiosity, which was suppressed by society. He wrote that the impulse for knowledge and investigation was a sublimated form of acquisition at least partially driven by voyeurism. In subsequent years, a host of other lesser-known psychoanalysts have concluded that curiosity can take the form of an intense drive, not unlike our sex drives. But just like sex, the results of the hunt can be hit or miss.

One of the first academic studies of vagabonds, "The Tramp as a Social Morbidity," published in 1907 by Vassar College professor Dr. Harriet C. B. Alexander, asserted that "the English-speaking race has developed because of its wandering tendencies." But it also condemned wandering types as societal "defectives." Alexander proposed that the "social remedies" for aspects of vagabondage included better housing, fair labor conditions, and improved sanitation and public health. "Society has created its vagabonds, as it has created other defective classes," he concluded.

While Alexander viewed the nomadic tendency as a product of society's shortcomings, another prominent study, "The Feebly Inhibited: Nomadism, or the Wandering Impulse, with Special Reference to Heredity; Inheritance of Temperament," published in 1915 by the Carnegie Institution, examined the hereditary aspect of wanderlust.

The report attempted to determine why persons differ in their capacity for remaining "quiet and satisfied for a long period in one place," and was authored by Charles Davenport, a prominent scientist and leader of the racist American eugenics movement. Underwritten by John D. Rockefeller, then the world's richest man, Davenport's research team studied a hundred families to shed light on why some people are satisfied to remain at home while others feel compelled to wander. (Imagine Bill Gates or Jeff Bezos commissioning something like this today!)

Davenport found that men were far more likely to be nomadic than women; there were 171 nomadic men among the 100 families to just 15 nomadic females. He asserted that there is an innate tendency to nomadism in the human race, but believed this predisposition was corrected by the "more intellectual part of the population" through their inhibitions.

Nomads, he claimed, suffered from "feeble inhibitions," which failed to put the brakes on their innate nomadic tendencies. The undertone of the paper is the notion that civilized, cultured people have the ability to control their wandering impulses, while more primitive and less intelligent dopes like me do not. And Davenport believed that genetics offered an explanation: "All the evidence supports the hypothesis that the nomadic impulse depends upon the absence of a simple sex-linked gene that determines 'domesticity.'"

Davenport also concluded, "Persons differ greatly in their capacity for remaining quiet and satisfied for a long period in one place," and claimed "Americans probably represent a selection of the more nomadic individuals of Europe."

Ralph Waldo Emerson concurred and thought this was a kind of national character flaw. "I think, there is a restlessness in our people, which argues want of character," he said.

A year later, J. H. Williams followed up on Davenport's study with one of his own, "The Intelligence of the Delinquent Boy," which studied 470 juvenile delinquents and their families to see if "nomadism" played a role in their wayward behavior. Williams found that nomadism or the "wandering impulse" was the inherent cause of about half of the truancy cases in the study. Researching the family members' tendencies to wander or stay put, he found that heredity was an important factor in predicting delinquency.

While 30 percent of the relatives of truants were deemed "nomadic," only 1 percent of the family members of non-truants were nomadic. "Hereditary nomadism is probably the chief contributing cause of at least 50 percent of cases in which truancy is the principal offense," Williams concluded.

Like Davenport, Williams thought that nomadism was a sex-linked trait that could be overcome by civilized people.

"The wandering instinct is a fundamental human instinct, which is, however, typically inhibited in intelligent adults of civilized peoples," he concluded.

In 1927, William J. Tinkle, a superbly surnamed Wisconsin academic, conducted a study of 150 families called "The Heredity of Habitual Wandering." Tinkle also believed that there was a strong hereditary aspect to wandering and noted that men were more likely to be nomadic than women. But he thought that the "limiting influence" on women was social and not biological. "Were it not for restraints laid upon women by society as well as their natural physical handicaps, we should see just as many wandering women as men…[but] most women will not give up their standing in society."

Tinkle attempted to define nomads by three characteristics. Nomads, he claimed, wandered impulsively, unreasonably, and habitually:

> In a normal individual, his impulses, if foolish or harmful, are inhibited by his reason; but not so in the nomad, if he gets the impulse to go. Most nomads will steal or beg when hungry… the trait being of such an unreasonable nature, it is usually hard for appeals to the reason to produce any effect.

> It is quite normal for one who has been confined at his post of labor to enjoy a trip for a change; but having returned [home] he appreciates his comfortable home and is more content with his job for having gone.

Tinkle believed that nomads didn't feel this same relief to return to their routine. He decided that the nomadic trait was linked to an independent, recessive factor not linked with intelligence. Tinkle ended with a cautionary note, hinting strongly that nomadism was a dangerous character trait. He said that more research was needed in order to keep the nomadically inclined from "joining the sordid ranks of tramps and criminals."

While Davenport and others were fixated on the absence of a 'domesticity gene' as an explanation for nomadism, geneticists in recent years have searched for answers in the opposite direction, investigating the possibility that some humans carry a so-called restless or nomadic gene. In 2013, *National Geographic* published a story about DRD4-7R, a variation (allele) of a gene carried by roughly 19 percent of all people and tied to curiosity and restlessness. Dozens of studies have associated this gene with novelty seeking and hyperactivity, and have found that people with 7R are more likely to engage in risky behavior, and generally crave movement, change, and adventure. Its effects on personality are more prominent in men.

Dr. Chuansheng Chen, a geneticist at the University of California, Irvine, is the lead author of a groundbreaking 1999 study that found 7R was significantly more common in historically migratory cultures than in settled ones. Using genetic data from 2,320 people from 39 different cultures culled from 12 different studies, the authors proved that populations that had moved far away from their ancient places of origin had a disproportionate number of 7R bearers compared to groups who stayed put. The fact that South American cultures like the fierce Yanomamö had the highest instance of 7R carriers reflects the great distance they migrated from Africa, where mankind originated.

The Mayo Clinic tests for the gene because it's closely linked to attention deficit hyperactivity disorder (ADHD). It estimates that 19.2 percent of us carry one copy of DRD4-7R (and just 3.7 percent carry two copies of it), while 65.1 percent carry another variant, DRD4-4R. 7Rs and 4Rs are on opposite sides of the novelty-seeking spectrum, according to a 2011 paper written by Dr. Luke Matthews, a professor of human evolutionary biology at Harvard University, and Dr. Paul Butler, a professor at Boston University's School of Medicine. They describe high-novelty-seeking 7Rs as "exploratory, impulsive, excitable, quick-tempered, and extravagant," while 4Rs are considered "rigid, prudent, stoic, reflective, staid, and slow-tempered."

Genes work together, so to divvy up the world into a 7R-versus-4R clash of cultures is an oversimplification of how our genes work. Humans have more than twenty thousand genes and each one has hundreds of variations, and it is the complex mosaic of genes we inherit that most accurately predicts behavior and personality traits. Geneticists have a hard enough time trying to isolate clearly diagnosable diseases; attempting to pinpoint the genetic source of something much more nebulous like wanderlust and novelty seeking is much harder.

But it's significant to note that 4R is more than three times as common as 7R. This statistic hints at the difficulty high-novelty seekers like me have functioning in a world that is run by people who are more prudent and cautious. Imagine if the world was run by free-spirited 7Rs, rather than practical and accountable 4Rs. The five-day workweek might be three or four. Every day would be casual Friday. Formal office environments might cease to exist. Western civilization might be completely different than it is now.

Authors of the aforementioned studies credit the preponderance of the 7R gene variant in migratory cultures largely to natural selection, which purges severely detrimental traits over time. Novelty seeking and exploratory behavior were beneficial traits in migratory societies. But in sedentary cultures, where resources are secured by cultivating a limited geographic space rather than exploiting new environments, those same traits were counterproductive.

In migratory cultures, the 7R gene would proliferate, as novelty seekers lived longer and had more children; in sedentary cultures, the 7R gene would be deselected and would die out. Novelty seekers have historically been skilled at adapting to change, so in cultures that have experienced generations of migration, 7R bearers have thrived.

This dynamic was corroborated by a 2008 University of Washington study of Ariaal pastoralists who live in resource-scarce northern Kenya. Scientists contrasted members of the tribe who are still nomadic with other members who have been settled for about thirty-five years. They found that nomadic 7Rs were healthier than settled 7Rs and asserted that this could be explained either because the gene was beneficial in a nomadic setting but not in settled communities or because the nomadic 7Rs were more selfish with their food. (In explaining the latter possibility, the authors cited a 2005 Hebrew University study that concluded that 7Rs are more selfish and less altruistic.)

Noting the strong connection between 7R and ADHD, which now affects some 3 to 5 percent of elementary school students in the U.S. and the U.K., Chen argues that this dysfunction may be emblematic of man's difficult human adaptation from the nomadic era. Then, having a high level of activity and attention diversion was beneficial; now, the ability to sit still and focus intently on a task is more useful to our highly structured, sedentary, modern society.

In a 2002 commentary on the impact of 7R, Henry Harpending and Gregory Cochran, anthropology professors at the University of Utah, noted that two of the best-known ethnographic studies of the twentieth century involved tribes at opposite ends of the 7R continuum. One report, called "The Harmless People," chronicled Africa's docile !Kung bushmen, who have few or no 7R bearers; the other, "The Fierce People," detailed the lives of South America's Yanomamö, who have a very high frequency of 7R. 7R bearers thrived in cultures (like that of the Yanomamö) where face-to-face male competition and violence proliferated, but not in more pacifist ones, like the !Kungs.

Warrior instincts might not seem particularly useful in modern societies, but the news isn't all bad for 7Rs. In 2013, the *Journal of Neuroscience* revealed that individuals carrying 7R lived longer, possibly because their hyperactivity and novelty-seeking tendency motivated them to exercise. In surveying Americans of European ancestry aged ninety and over, they found that this "oldest-old" population was 66 percent more likely to carry 7R than the control group, comprised of individuals aged seven to forty-five. Both men and women with 7R older than ninety reported higher levels of physical activity than those without it, suggesting that while hyperactivity might be a burden in youth, it could be an advantage in old age.

Chen contends that studying 7R and other individual gene variants in isolation isn't optimal, because genes work together. Still, he insists that any personality trait, including restlessness, has a strong hereditary component. "Sixty to seventy percent of variances in personality traits can be explained by genetic factors," he says.

A study of 3,687 pairs of seven-year-old twins in the UK published in the *Journal of Child Psychology and Psychiatry* in 2005 found that heritability was even higher—81 percent—for callous, unemotional traits that are considered an early warning sign of psychopathic behavior. But oddly enough, milder antisocial behavior traits were found to be 70 percent environmental and only 30 percent genetic. We don't know what the heritability rate is for novelty seeking and exploratory behavior and so the genetic influence could be anywhere from moderate to extreme. I have moved seventeen times among eight U.S. states and four countries since graduating from college. My resume is a hot mess. I've been a transient, living out of a suitcase for months at a time on seven occasions, and these brief nomadic forays have been the happiest times of my life. But coming home has always been a problem. When I'm stuck in one place, I'm like a junkie in need of a fix.

In my twenties, I couldn't or wouldn't sit still. Whenever my bank account hit $10,000, I tendered my resignation and hit the road. At thirty, I joined the Foreign Service; a career that I naively imagined would be like a halfway house for wayward travelers. After five years and postings in four countries, I realized that moving every two to three years wasn't enough stimulation for me.

At thirty-three, I was diagnosed with Multiple Sclerosis after a year of doctor's visits and uncertainty. The diagnosis came as a kind of relief, because I feared that I had ALS or another terminal illness. But the fatigue was so extreme at times that I could barely go for a short walk, let alone embark on a big trip. The disease went into remission after several years of suffering and the reprieve gave me a convenient new excuse to travel. My illness reminded me that there is no guarantee that I'll be healthy enough to explore later on.

In my case, it would be easy to conclude that I inherited my wanderlust from my parents, both of whom were frequent, though not extreme, travelers well into their retirement years. But genetics are never straightforward. I have five brothers with varying degrees of wanderlust, ranging from severe to very moderate. Is it our genetics or our experiences or a combination of the two that make us different?

In his delightful book, *Birding Without Borders: An Obsession, a Quest, and the Biggest Year in the World*, Noah Strycker makes an important observation about birds that may well apply to the wanderlust-afflicted. Strycker reports that the German word for the migratory instinct of birds—*zugunruhe*—combines the words zug (move or migration) and unruhe (restlessness).

He writes, "researchers have shown, under controlled conditions that caged songbirds try to hop, flap, and jump in the same compass direction as they would naturally migrate. Birds become physically restless during migration season…in other words birds are programmed to move."

A study published in 1950, "Novelty and Curiosity as Determinants of Exploratory Behaviour," written by Daniel Berlyne, a professor of psychology at the University of St. Andrews, posits that novelty may hold the key to understanding human motivations. "Few human impulses are more inexorable than the urge to escape from monotony and boredom to some new form of stimulation," he wrote.

Berlyne observed twelve male albino rats in a maze and found that curiosity was more closely related to anxiety than previously known. Anything novel placed into the maze excited fear or curiosity in the rats, but oftentimes the rats appeared to be wavering between the two.

Numerous other studies have shown that rats demonstrate a preference for the less familiar of two arms of a maze, and are willing to endure electrical shocks to explore novel stimuli unrelated to food or water. Pavlov found in 1927 that his dogs would turn toward any unusual sight or sound and attributed this to an investigatory reflex. In the 1950s, researchers found that monkeys kept in shielded cages demonstrated behavior that illustrated their preference to be able to see out of windows. And the longer the monkeys were deprived of light in a box, the more they craved visual stimulation.

In his study involving rats, Berlyne remarked that fear and curiosity were alike in that they were both drives that inspired an organism to want to put an end to them. That is, no person, rat, or other animal wants to live in a state of fear or unsatisfied curiosity. But the behavior associated with curiosity and fear differed dramatically—one inspired approach and the other withdrawal.

Perhaps we're all born with an innate curiosity that makes us prone to wander. But there is this fine line between fear and curiosity that makes us respond differently. Someone who has an early negative experience on a trip—say they were robbed in Venice or got sick in Dubai—may have their innate wanderlust extinguished. But the inverse will happen to someone who has more positive experiences.

Don Parrish got hooked on travel after the formative experience he had in Germany back in 1965. He's certain that he has the explorer's gene, and says the proof is in his family tree. Parrish claims five ancestors who came to the New World on the *Mayflower*, and says that one of his relations is Jan Vigne, the first boy born in

Manhattan, in 1624. Parrish's first European ancestor was an interpreter for the French explorer Samuel de Champlain.

"And I have Mohawk Indian ancestors via Jacques Hertel [Champlain's interpreter]," he says. "So that means my ancestors came to the New World from Asia across the Bering Strait about twelve thousand years ago and became the 'Indians.'"

After reading everything I could find about DRD4-7R, I had to know if I had it. Convincing a doctor to write me a prescription for the Mayo Clinic's DRD4 genetic test took some doing, but when I turned up at my local Quest Diagnostics lab in Bend, Oregon, with the appropriate requisition forms one bright spring morning, I had never been more excited about giving blood.

After the phlebotomist—who had never heard of DRD4 or the Mayo Clinic—did her job, I sat in the chair for an extra minute examining three milliliter-sized vials of my blood she had placed on the desk. Was there something there in my blood predisposing me to wander the earth?

I've never met another obsessive traveler who has gone through the trouble and expense of being tested for 7R, but most of the travelers I interviewed for this book believe that there is at least some genetic component to their restlessness. William said he inherited his love of travel from his mother.

Many say that their hunger to explore is an innate part of them, something they are stuck with for better or worse. Some of us are genetically more likely to be restless, but our fate is far from predetermined at birth. We need sparks and opportunities for the novelty-seeking trait to flourish and go into overdrive. In many cases, all it takes is just one trip and we're hooked or, if things go wrong, put off forever.

CHAPTER 8

◇◇◇◇◇◇◇◇

Destination Palmyra: "I'm In Regardless of Price."

You cannot avoid paradise.
You can only avoid seeking it.

—CHARLOTTE JOKO BECK

Palmyra is a typically off-limits atoll a thousand miles south of Hawaii and 5,400 miles away from the nearest continent that's privately owned by the Nature Conservancy (TNC), a conservation nonprofit. The twelve-square-kilometer island is the United States' only "unorganized incorporated territory," which means that federal law gives the president the authority to administer the island but there is no act of Congress specifying how the place should be governed.

Only a handful of TNC researchers live in this tropical paradise at any given time, and few tourists visit because of the expense and hassle of chartering a flight or a boat (it's a five-to-seven-day sail from Honolulu) and obtaining the necessary permits. But it's firmly on the radar of country collectors because it's a tough mark on the club lists.

Boasting some fifteen thousand acres of magnificent coral reefs, Palmyra has one of the richest marine ecosystems in the world. It's a kind of Shangri-la for wildlife viewing, particularly for birders looking for red-footed, brown, and masked boobies, sooty terns, black noddies, and great frigate birds, among many other amusingly named birds.

In the spring of 2016, William Baekeland pulled off an extreme travel coup by securing Palmyra permits for a small group of top travelers, including Don Parish, Bob Bonifas, and Bruno Rodi, a successful Canadian-Italian entrepreneur. The plan was to fly to the island on a private jet with William; then TNC conservation staff would lead them on a private tour.

They paid William between $18,000 and $25,000 each to spend six hours on the island. Baekeland told Bonifas, the CEO and founder of an alarm detection service company in Chicago with three hundred employees, in an email that they would be able to visit Palmyra under a "philanthropic scheme, which my family are doing with TNC." Baekeland told Bonifas that the price of the visit was $12,500 but added that he "strongly recommended" he add a $10,000 donation to TNC.

"The reason I am able to travel there is because of my family's planned giving arrangements with the owners of the island for ongoing conservation work," Baekeland wrote. "Passengers arriving by air is strictly on the basis of being involved in philanthropy of some sort, or scientific work, or other official business. I am approved to travel, no problem, but even any guests of mine are not 100% my choice. The owners have final say, and the US Fish and Wildlife Service have additional say in the matter."

William promised them an official tour of the TNC station, along with a boat tour of the lagoon, visiting coral reefs and islets. "You can snorkel if you wish, they have shower facilities on the island," he wrote. "Lunch/and/or dinner will be served at the island station."

Bob Bonifas

At the time, Bonifas had less than thirty places to visit on MTP's 874-place list and Palmyra was one of his remaining targets, so he wrote Baekeland on January 21, 2016, "I'm in regardless of price." Bonifas calls himself a "class A personality" who is happiest when he's at his lake home in Wisconsin. Though they met for the first time in Afghanistan, he lives just ten miles from Don Parrish in Chicago's western suburbs. Each has held the number-one ranking on MTP at various points in the last few years.

Bonifas described his approach to moving up the MTP list in the *Counting Countries* podcast as "playing a game." When he first started to count countries a little over a decade ago, it was easy. "You're looking at the guys ahead of you, you knock out twenty places on a trip and you can pop over a hundred people on the list so it was pretty rewarding back when travel was easy," he said. "But of the places I have left now, you can't fly into them, you can't go in without government permission. They're terribly difficult places. You spend a lot of time on boats and you get nothing in return."

By these tough standards, the Palmyra trip seemed straightforward at the time. Bonifas left Chicago on Thursday, March 31, flying to Honolulu, and then on to Palmyra on Friday, and was back in Chicago by Saturday, April 2. Just five days after returning to Chicago, Bonifas received an email from TNC's Honolulu-based assistant director of philanthropy, whom I'll call Ms. Lorenzi since she declined to be interviewed, inviting him to make a donation and return to Palmyra for a longer visit. In her message, she implied that they didn't see much due to the brief nature of their visit. "I'm glad you got to check off another box," she wrote, referring to the quest to complete the MTP list.

As they corresponded, Bonifas learned that Baekeland had charged different travelers varying prices for the trip and that William hadn't passed on the $10,000-per-person "donations" that were intended for TNC. "It is troublesome in the extreme that William asked some of you for a donation, but so far has held onto it," Lorenzi wrote.

William on Palmyra Atoll

Baekeland subsequently told Lorenzi that his family would consider a multi-year gift of $1 million. She went to New York to meet with him in mid-September 2016 and he promised to make the first donation as soon as he returned to Ireland the day after their meeting. But William dragged his feet with a host of creative excuses and Lorenzi was reluctant to push him too hard, as he had told her that his sister had recently died. In a December 16 email, Lorenzi informed Bonifas, "I sent him [Baekeland] a letter to give to his bank that he said was impounding the funds because they confused Palmyra Atoll with Palmyra, Syria, and they were concerned about funding terrorism."

Lorenzi and TNC eventually gave up and Bonifas started to wonder if perhaps Baekeland was crooked. Five months after the failed Bouvet trip, in November 2015, Baekeland sent a message to Bonifas offering him a spot on a nine-day private yacht trip he was organizing to Trindade and Martin Vaz, a pair of stunning, volcanic islands with rocky cliffs that are uninhabited save for a small contingent of Brazilian Navy personnel located some 680 miles off the coast of Brazil. William offered Bonifas a shared cabin on board a fifty-eight-foot yacht for $11,545 but floated the possibility of a private cabin for $18,742.

"My journey to these islands is the first foreign visit in a long time," Baekeland wrote on November 1. "Permission has come from two levels of Brazilian government—the navy and environmental agency."

Bonifas was impressed and made a $6,000 deposit. Two weeks later, he committed to another trip William offered to Wake Island and Johnston Atoll, a lonely outpost on his MTP to-do list that's a rarely visited, unincorporated U.S. territory administered by the United States Fish and Wildlife Service. Bonifas paid the full cost of this trip—$14,000—on November 23, 2015. Then on December 20, Bonifas signed up and paid in full ($8,900) for a third Baekeland charter trip, this time to the Chilean island of San Félix in the Desventuradas Islands, another obscure spot on the MTP list that's home to a lonely military base and no permanent residents.

On February 13, 2016, just weeks before the Palmyra trip, William postponed the Desventuradas trip, two days prior to its start.

"This morning I have bad news," he wrote. "The commander of the Chilean Armada is flying on this day now and we are bumped to the bottom of their priority list." He claimed that permission hadn't been revoked, and wrote, "the islands are too rare and unique to give up over because [sic] of an issue like this."

At least one member of the small group had already traveled from the United States to Santiago, Chile. Three days later and just days before the Johnston Atoll trip, Baekeland wrote Bonifas to say that the U.S. government had revoked permission to land on Johnston Atoll, asserting that it had withdrawn the personnel from the island who were going to show them around. "As we know from the island staff I know, [sic] the actual reason was ICBM missile tests going on that month," he wrote.

Baekeland held out the possibility that the trip might be rescheduled for a later date and there was no talk of refunds. And so, by the time Lorenzi informed him that Baekeland hadn't passed on their TNC donations, Bonifas suspected that something was amiss.

On June 24, 2016, William invited Bob on a small private boat excursion he was planning to Rockall Island—the big uninhabited rock off the coast of Ireland that David Langan found so difficult to reach out and touch. Bonifas was very leery of Baekeland by this point, but Rockall was one of his remaining MTP targets, so he agreed to go. In one email regarding the trip, Bonifas described himself as someone who "lived my life doing the difficult and the uncomfortable and I survived."

But when Bonifas insisted on securing refunds for the three cancelled trips first, Baekeland balked and then ultimately revoked Bob's invitation for the trip. In his final email to Bonifas on June 24, 2017, Baekeland promised trip refunds, but coolly concluded, "With respect to all other matters and communication, I am advised not to prejudice my position. Accordingly, all further correspondence with myself should be via lawyers. William S. Baekeland."

"I've been in business for sixty years," Bonifas told me. "But I've never been screwed like this before. I should have woken up sooner. I was smelling all kinds of dead rats."

CHAPTER 9

◇◇◇◇◇◇◇◇

Evolution of the
Modern Supertramp

Civilization is what makes you sick.

—Paul Gauguin

The fact that travel is, at least for some, a competitive endeavor shows how far we've shifted on the evolutionary spectrum from the days when man traveled as a means of survival. Homo sapiens evolved in Africa some two hundred thousand years ago. These early humans didn't start to walk out of Africa for another eighty thousand years or so. Men were hunter-gatherers until the advent of sedentary agriculture, which began as early as 12,000 B.C. in some places, like the Levant, and as recently as 5,000 B.C. in the Americas.

The Natufians founded Jericho, widely considered the world's first city, around 12,000 B.C. But researchers have recently concluded that the Natufians didn't engage in agriculture for another two thousand years. Therefore, the long-held notion that men settled down and formed communities simply to guarantee their food source is now in question. We don't know what compelled the Natufians and other nomadic groups to form stable communities, but archaeologists and historians have put forward dozens of theories, some more plausible than others.

Felipe Fernández-Armesto, a history professor at the University of Notre Dame, explained several of these possibilities in his book, *Civilizations: Culture, Ambition, and the Transformation of Nature*. The most likely theory may be that climactic change forced nomads to establish settlements in temperate zones. Perhaps, but surely the most entertaining theory is that men settled because they wanted to brew and consume beer, and the former is impossible without a base. It's also possible that early nomads discovered that sedentary life was more conducive to mating. Food, beer, and sex must have been high on the list of priorities for men and women in any region at any time in history.

While we don't know exactly why humans started to settle, we do know that the transition from nomadism to sedentism didn't pay immediate dividends. Bill Bryson noted in his book *At Home: A Short History of Private Life* that nomads ate healthier and were less prone to illness.

"Sedentism meant poorer diets, more illness, lots of toothache and gum disease, and earlier deaths," he wrote. "What is truly extraordinary is that these are all still factors in our lives today."

Philip Carl Salzman is a professor of anthropology at McGill University who has studied nomads since he lived with a nomadic tribe in Balochistan in the seventies as part of his dissertation research. Salzman says that historically there have been three types of nomads: hunter-gatherers, pastoralists (who move to find pasture for their animals), and occupational groups like the Roma, who make their living on the road as traders, laborers, musicians, and in other fields.

Traditional nomads have wandered for two primary reasons: to make a living and for defense. Groups who stay on the move can avoid being conquered, subjugated, or persecuted.

In modern times, nomads have been stigmatized and lionized in equal measure. We romanticize nomads because we admire their freedom. The promise of the American West as a new frontier has long been connected to this notion that it is a wide-open space where Native Americans, cowboys, and hoboes roam the land, free from societal norms. The nineteenth-century poet, editor, and diplomat James Russell Lowell nicely summed up our national psyche when he said, "The American is nomadic in religion, in ideas, in morals, and leaves his faith and opinions with as much indifference as the house in which he lives."

A. M. Khazanov, in his book *Nomads and the Outside World*, wrote that men have been romanticizing nomadic life since at least the fifth century B.C., when Herodotus wrote an idealized description of nomadic Scythians.

But nomadic groups have also long been derided as uncivilized, shifty, prone to crime, and worse. The classic example of a stigmatized group is the Roma, a traditionally nomadic ethnic group that migrated from India to Europe about a thousand years ago. Hitler exterminated more than one hundred thousand Roma in concentration camps during World War II, and they remain marginalized and persecuted to this day.

Nomads have been viewed in a derogatory light since biblical times. In the book of Genesis, Cain was condemned to be a "fugitive and wanderer of the earth" for murdering his brother, Abel. Moses and the Israelites wandered in the desert for forty years as a punishment from God for their faithlessness. The legend of the Wandering Jew condemned to walk the earth until the Second Coming has endured for centuries. And so has the myth of the *Flying Dutchman*, a ghost ship that can never reach port and is condemned to sail the oceans in perpetuity.

Felipe Fernández-Armesto debunked the long-held notion that nomadic groups cannot be civilized, pointing to the nomadic Scythians, who created enduring works of art, built impressive structures, and established sophisticated political and economic systems in modern- day Iran starting in the ninth century B.C.

Fernández-Armesto asserts in *The World: A History* that nomads and settled farmers engaged in a clash of cultures during the Middle Ages, defined by mutual revulsion and outright warfare. Nomads couldn't manufacture commodities such as tea, fruit, and grain, so they raided settled communities to plunder these items.

"There is no moral difference between settled and nomadic lifeways," Fernández-Armesto says. "Each community, however, tended to see the other as morally inferior."

In many ways, popular opinion about itinerant people hasn't changed much over the centuries. An article on the arrival of a group of Zingari gypsies in New York, which appeared in the *New York Times* on April 3, 1870, neatly captured the schizophrenic vox populi of the time, categorizing nomads as a breed worthy of both envy and scorn. The author referred to their "apparent freedom from the myriad cares which harass and oppress us in the modern world," but also implied that nomads were dishonest, unfaithful to their wives, and had criminal tendencies.

"[The nomad] can never be made to be what we call a 'useful member of society.' There is a mystic drop in his blood which will keep him a wanderer."

An article with the headline "The Causes of Vagabondage" which first appeared in the influential (and now long-defunct) *Century Magazine* and was reprinted in the *New York Times* on December 22, 1895, sheds more light on the perception of wanderlust at the time. The article identified five "principal causes" of vagabondage without defining the term itself.

1. The love of liquor
2. Wanderlust—the love of wandering
3. The county jail
4. The tough and rough element in the villages and towns
5. The comparatively innocent but misguided pupils of the reform school

"The Feebly Inhibited," the Carnegie Institution study of nomadism published in 1915, is proof the lifestyle was considered an inherited character flaw as recently as a century ago. Well- bred, cultured people could overcome man's innate desire to wander, but primitive, less-cultured people could not.

Still, some, including the Irish playwright George Bernard Shaw, retained a sort of admiration for wanderers and tramps. Shaw helped pluck W. H. Davies, the author of *The Autobiography of a Super-Tramp*, out of obscurity in 1905. Davies sent Shaw a copy of his self- published memoir, detailing his years tramping around North America and Britain, and Shaw liked it enough to provide a blurb and help him get it published.

A 1993 mini-review of the book, written by Jonathan Raban in the *New York Times*, describes Davies as a "thief and a drunk" who also wrote poems that saved him from homelessness. Shaw helped "turn the 34-year-old tramp into an overnight celebrity. He died in 1940, a rubicund old lion with a young wife, a huge circle of admirers and a secure place in the anthologies."

Purely elective, individual nomadism—what the peripatetic writer Bruce Chatwin called "neurotic" nomadism—didn't take off in the United States until the sixties and seventies, as legions of baby boomers—some dodging the draft, others simply indulging their wanderlust—dropped out of the rat race and drifted around the world, sometimes for years at a time. The global travel industry expanded tenfold in the sixties, with the total number of international trips exploding from 25 to 250 million during the decade.

Ed Buryn's influential book *Vagabonding in Europe and North Africa*, a surprise bestseller for HarperCollins in 1971, captured the zeitgeist of this era with exhortations to reject the "rising tide of obscene tourism" and see the world as a "free person, a vagabond."

"The world doesn't end when you decide to do what you want to do, it merely begins," he wrote. "All through history, vagabonds have traversed the Earth living the best lives ever known."

Thirty years later, Rolf Potts's *Vagabonding: An Uncommon Guide to the Art of Long-Term World Travel* inspired a new generation of would-be nomads to travel slower, longer, and deeper. "Vagabonding is about using the prosperity and possibility of the information age to increase your personal options instead of your personal possessions," Potts wrote.

The nature of work has changed dramatically in recent years. Corporate culture has rapidly transitioned toward a gig economy, where employers have more contractors and freelancers than permanent employees. Researchers project that by 2030, freelancers may outnumber full-timers. That dynamic should free up more people to be mobile or even fully nomadic. But at the moment, many still feel an intense societal pressure to plant roots because settling down has become synonymous with growing up.

When Lainie Liberti, a free-spirited single mom and former advertising executive who blogs about family travel, took her ten-year-old son out of school to travel the world for a year, most in her peer group were supportive.

"A one-year break is socially acceptable," she says. "But when the one-year sabbatical turns into your lifestyle, people just think you're irresponsible and need to settle down."

Very early on in my professional career I knew that I would need to find a way to contain my wandering impulse if I wanted to be a productive member of polite society. My parents—reared during the Great Depression—had invested so much in my education. I couldn't just be a traveling bum. I had to find a career that involved travel. Preferably lots of it. William was obviously a kindred spirit. Was he the man of leisure he claimed to be, or just a young man looking for a way to make a career out of his wanderlust?

CHAPTER 10

◇◇◇◇◇◇◇◇◇◇

The Dashing Kim Il Sung University Grad

I sought voyages to disperse enchant-
ments that had colonized my mind.

—Arthur Rimbaud

As 2016 drew to a close, William was in arrears to a number of top travelers, but few of them were comparing notes about their experiences because of the culture of discretion and secrecy among the ranks of elite country collectors. Bizas, whom William owed €19,000 by this point, says that few were complaining out loud because no one wanted to be taken off of Baekeland's trip invite list. Despite the rash of cancellations, William continued to quietly build his profile and client list. On September 5, 2016, he participated in a Skype interview with Ric Gazarian, the host of the *Counting Countries* podcast, who introduced him as a young man of twenty-three who had "made his way to over three quarters of the world's countries."

In the interview, Baekeland claimed that he traveled to Prague more than a hundred times in his youth for harpsichord lessons after his Czech instructor was too ill to teach him in the UK. He revealed that he developed an interest in visiting offbeat parts of the world through a three-thousand-page fact book he read as a teenager. And he claimed that he started to visit "difficult" countries like Chad and the Central African Republic at age eighteen.

"I'm traveling to every country in the world," he said.

Baekeland sounded a bit hesitant, and very upper crust, almost like a member of the royal family reluctantly granting an interview. William's responses were always plausible but brief and not very revealing. Thirty-seven minutes into the interview, Gazarian finally asked him the obvious question. "This is obviously a pretty big financial commitment. How are you managing to do this in terms of work?"

William deftly batted the question away without really answering it, simply saying, "I've been fortunate enough to be able to do this," before changing the topic to his academic career. Gazarian didn't follow up, presumably because he and everyone else in the world of elite travel knew that William was a billionaire.

Even though William didn't detail his financial situation, his answers left no doubt that he came from money. Baekeland said that he always stayed in the best hotels possible, preferably heritage hotels, because they tend to have the best security. William said that his favorite hotel is the historic Royal Hawaiian Hotel, known as the Pink Palace, on Waikiki Beach, which he said his family has visited every year since it opened in 1927.

"I don't have a website or blog or anything like that," Baekeland said. "I don't publicize my travels in any way and I don't intend to either."

He sounded like the opposite of a salesman, and Gazarian, who came off like an admiring fan, gushed in conclusion, "It's amazing to hear how much of the world he's seen at such a young age."

Two weeks later, William's low-key extreme travel media tour continued, as Harry Mitsidis published an interview with him in the September 20 issue of the NomadMania newsletter that was surreally devoted to "safety online." Mitsidis introduced Baekeland as "not your average 23-year-old" and concluded he was "most probably the youngest of the world's truly global explorers." He would later describe William in his book as a young man who "could move mountains, move borders, and move obstacles, to expand the world and its horizons." Together, Mitsidis believed he and Baekeland could "make the world larger than it has ever been, and then work toward conquering its pieces, thereby rendering it small again."

William claimed in the newsletter interview that he grew up in London but spent a lot of time during his childhood in South Africa, the United States, Switzerland, and Spain. He mentioned that he was "busy" writing a book about Norwegian Antarctica and that he had completed exchange programs in Finland and at Kim Il Sung University in North Korea of all places, where he allegedly studied North Korean government and politics.

"My motivation for this [travel] has always been to give myself first-hand understanding of the things I wish to learn about," he said.

Baekeland said that his mother traveled to almost all of the countries of Africa and Oceania and said that his grandmother went on a trip around the world in the 1930s. "So you could say it is in the blood, my desire to travel is not a surprise to them," he said.

Mitsidis asked about Baekeland's (twelve-thousand-place) list of destinations and he mentioned Kapingamarangi, as one of the places on his wish list. "It's a rather isolated atoll in Micronesia which has a population of about 500 people and in theory Spain still has a legal basis for claiming its sovereignty," he said. "I already tried to go there but my attempt fell through. I'll try again."

williambaekeland • Following

williambaekeland The camel market of el Fasher, Darfur, Sudan
haydzarantz When did you go there?
williambaekeland @haydzarantz Late 2016
haydzarantz @williambaekeland My, that was recent.
williambaekeland @haydzarantz October 2016 - I had a fun time.

22 likes
FEBRUARY 10, 2017

Add a comment...

When asked about his more immediate travel plans, Baekeland unfurled an extraordinary laundry list of peculiar destinations, many of them places big-time country collectors dream of:

> I will be in South Sudan and then North Sudan and Darfur, after that I will go to South America to visit Chile and Brazil and a few islands around there, and then over to Africa, and the Himalayas to reach a number of the highest mountains by helicopter, including the remote Kingdom of Lo Manthang, then it's

back to The Americas. In January I'm going to Clipperton Island and then some more of the islands of the Pacific such as Tokelau. In March I'm off to the Victoria Falls, then on the Rovos Rail 'Pride of Africa' train to Pretoria and then [I'll] drive across Lesotho to Durban from where I'm taking a cruise on a luxury French ship from Durban to the Seychelles via the Iles Eparses, Madagascar and the famed Atoll of Aldabra.

William en route to Saint Pierre and Miquelon Islands

The pair of interviews set the stage for William's 2016 Christmas card, in which he detailed the deaths of his sisters, Muguette and Ariadne, along with a seven-nine-page photo slideshow of his year in travel. Here are some excerpts:

2016 has been an indescribably bad and difficult year for both myself and my family. It is impossible to describe the whirlpool of emotion and feelings following the loss of both of my sisters. After eight months of intensive care support, it was finally realised at the end of August that it was the right time to withdraw this from Muguette. I was travelling in Canada at the time and immediately flew to New York City to be there for the end. She was unconscious and unresponsive for the entire eight-month period. She lived a short but engaging life. A simple closed-casket service was held in Manhattan for a small audience, limed [sic] to immediate family and close personal staff... The only piece of music of [sic] selected was 'Abide with Me', played on the organ. I lost my second sister, Ariadne, to weariness of life in October. It is a second tragedy impossible to describe. It came suddenly, forcing me to travel between continents again with hours of notice. Her funeral was held the same as Muguette's, also with 'Abide with Me'.

These events, and the events surrounding them have been incredibly challenging and force you to deal with problems head on. They bring out the best of people, but also the worst forms of greed in others, and this is very hard to face.

I am incredibly grateful to the huge number of people who have been supportive in the last month, and indeed year. I am still working on replying to the countless cards and letters and emails, by the New Year I shall have completed that. I also complete this task on behalf of my mother, who has been very unwell with pneumonia and sadness. To the many of you who know her well, your continued kindness is very gratefully received.

TRAVEL

An intensive travel schedule this year has helped significantly with all of the challenges faced during this past year. I've made multiple extended international trips, several sea voyages, a few 'pioneering' adventures as well as close to one hundred crossings between Ireland and the UK totally. I am attaching a PDF version of a slideshow of my year in travel, with a few select photos from some, but not all, of the places visited. A visual is better all round than long text at this busy time of year.

Two voyage which was [sic] especially memorable were, without a doubt, the crossing of Russia's North East Passage from East to West onboard the legendary icebreaker "KAPITAN KHLEBNIKOV" and the helicopter expedition around the Himalayas. During the

North East Passage expedition, my fellow
travellers and I explored Chukotka, Wrangel
Island, [the] New Siberian Islands, Severnaya
[Zemlya], Novaya [Zemlya], an unscheduled
long stop in Murmansk and, finally, Svalbard,
where a fun day trip to the abandoned Russian
town of Pyramiden was made. The voyage was
my seventh around the world journey, along
the following route:

Dublin
Frankfurt
Anchorage (Condor Airlines, fly-
ing the northern route, close to the
North Pole) Kodiak Island
Anadyr (Charter flight by Miami
Air International from Anchorage to
Anadyr) Russian North East Passage
Svalbad [sic]
Oslo
Dublin

In November I continued as planned with
travelling to Nepal to visit a number of the tall-
est mountains in the world, as well as several
other sites of outstanding scenic interest and
the seldom-visited former Kingdom of Lo in
Upper Mustang. During my stay in Mustang
I obtained a number of outstanding large
pieces of Tibetian artwork and several trea-

sured items belonging to the Royal Household in Manthang.

I leave you with a few travel statistics:

306 flights totally
6 continents
163 UN Countries totally
237 Travelers['] Century
Club countries totally
469 Most Traveled People countries totally Ranked No. 1 in Ireland,
by www.thebesttravelled.com
627 The Best Travelled countries totally

I hope that you all have a Merry Christmas and I wish you all the best for the coming 2017.

My very warmest wishes,

William S. Baekeland

In the accompanying slideshow, Baekeland advertised his dizzying jet-set lifestyle. There were aerial views of Barbuda, Chile's Atacama Desert, Monaco, where he got a private tour of a botanical garden, Mount Everest, and Niihau, Hawaii's forbidden island. In a snapshot from Venezuela's Isla de Aves, where he and a small group of top travelers toured the island by private yacht, he noted in the caption that he received a copy of the Venezuelan *Little Red Book on Socialism*. One photo of him in a Namibian ghost town shows him beaming, if a bit dorky, wearing an oversized sun hat, white oxford shirt, a khaki blazer with double pockets on each side, shorts, sandals, and sunglasses attached to a pair of Croakies.

A photo of young William looking dashing in a tuxedo, purportedly taken on his twenty-third birthday on board the *MS Silver Cloud* off the coast of Angola, bears a fun caption. "I had forgotten it was my birthday. The crew decorated my stateroom in balloons and banners. During the evening dinner the entire restaurant staff lined up to sing 'Happy Birthday' and presented a cake with candles."

March 8th 2016 - A candid shot taken on my 23rd birthday, off the coast of Lobito, Angola – onboard MS SILVER CLOUD

I had forgotten it was my birthday. The crew decorated my stateroom in balloons and banners. During the evening dinner the entire restaurant staff lined up to sing 'Happy Birthday' and presented a cake with candles.

Other shots highlighted his affinity for offbeat sightseeing. There were depictions of visits to deserted beaches in São Tomé, a shoe-making factory in Transnistria, a breakaway region of Moldova, an excursion to the northern most Stalin statue in the world, and a visit to Juba, South Sudan, which he called "unsafe" and "run down." He claimed to have explored Mount Everest in a "completely unique way," landing in a helicopter close to the 29,029-foot summit. And, on the less glamorous front, there was the "grim" fish market of Port Sudan, of which he remarked, "I shall not visit such a place again during my travels."

Mitsidis, who traveled with William in the Russian Arctic, Sudan, the Central African Republic, and a host of other places, aptly summed up what travelers thought they knew about the unbelievable young Brit after learning that he was also a pilot in his book:

> So he is not only a traveler, not only a trip organizer, a harpsichord and piano player, a manager of estates in Scotland, an amateur painter, an opera lover, a fantastic dresser and an eclectic vegan, he is also a knowledgeable meteorologist and a semi-professional pilot too. Is there anything this young man cannot do?

William in Sudan

CHAPTER 11

◇◇◇◇◇◇◇◇

Escape

Homesickness is a feeling many know and suf-
fer from; I on the other hand feel a pain less well
known, and its name is 'Outsickness.' When the
snow melts, the stork arises, and the first steam-
ships race off, then I feel the painful travel unrest.

—HANS CHRISTIAN ANDERSEN

Paul Salopek is a nomadic National Geographic Explorer who is more than seven years into a 21,000-mile "Out of Eden" walk that will take him from Ethiopia to Tierra del Fuego, retracing the path of human migration out of Africa in an epic journey that could take a decade or more. It's an extraordinary adventure, and Salopek says the journey has changed his view on the essential nature of movement. "Once you've been out walking around the world, to be travelling sitting down on your ass all the time seems ridiculous," he says. "It's hard for me to take anybody who travels sitting down on their ass very seriously any more, having walked several thousand miles out of Africa."

Salopek believes that humans aren't hardwired to be as sedentary as most of us are, and he's not alone. Bruce Chatwin said that we are all travelers by birth and argued that without change, our "brains and bodies rot." Richard Grant, in his 2003 study of nomads in the American West, *American Nomads*, wrote that freedom was "impossible and meaningless within the confines of sedentary society."

Researchers estimate that, on average, Americans spend more than half of their waking hours sitting down, a depressing reality that also has dangerous health consequences. This dynamic, coupled with the staggering amount of time many Americans spend commuting alone in their cars, adds up to a routine that is alienating for some but positively hellish for novelty seekers. Travel represents freedom from that prison. It's an indulgence and an avenue to flee from a job, a relationship, society, or oneself. In far-flung locales, one can reinvent oneself free from the confines of established social and familial bonds.

As long as work has existed, people have dreamed about quitting their jobs to go off traveling. But in an era where so many of us spend our workdays online or on the phone, and have jobs where it's hard to see the fruits of our labor, it can be difficult to find meaning in our work.

Nina Sedano, a German extreme traveler in her fifties who is ranked eighty-fourth on TBT/NomadMania, is one of the world's most traveled women, having visited all 193 UN countries. At thirty-six, she had already worked for Visa resolving customer disputes for fourteen years. But her colleagues were bilious and abusive. She spent many of her workdays indulging in what the Germans call

"*Sehnsucht*" (which can be translated literally as "seeing addiction"), essentially yearning for far-off places.

One day, nearly twenty years ago after one of her colleagues traduced her, she decided that she had had enough of the office life. Sedano quit her job and spent most of the next nine years traveling to every country on the planet.

"If my colleagues hadn't been so nasty, if I wasn't so fed up with my job, I don't think I would have ever traveled so much," she said.

The desire for escape, however, isn't always tied to hating one's job, boss, or colleagues.

Maurice Farber argued that part of the motivation to travel could be chalked up to "basic curiosity" and "exploratory drive," while noting that travel was also attractive to some because it was perceived as glamorous and carried the "weight of social prestige."

"Often the stereotype of a place arouses far more pleasure as an anticipatory response than the place itself," he wrote. "Candid travelers will sometimes admit that to say, 'Next week I shall be in Cairo,' involves a degree of gratification never reached in Cairo itself."

Farber detailed how travel frees us from our social inhibitions, allowing us to divulge our innermost fears and secrets to strangers. By contrast, in our ordinary lives, we feel the need to "keep up appearances" in our peer group, which causes loneliness as we fail to confide in others. Arrival in a foreign country often brings "euphoria and exhilaration" but the high, Farber wrote, doesn't last:

> We often find, particularly in those who spend considerable time abroad, that there is a profound discontent with their everyday lives. Sometimes merely a dull and routine job is involved. More frequently, inter-personal rela-

tions are found to be acutely unsatisfactory…
It is not improbable that even among normally
functioning people, the presence of an intense
passion to travel or live abroad as contrasted
with the widespread milder desire, [sic] is associated with a disturbed personality.

Nearly two decades later, in 1972, G. Raymond Babineau, a professor of psychiatry at the University of Rochester, picked up on this theme in his study, "The Compulsive Border Crosser," which focused on how fragile and emotionally unstable people sometimes travel compulsively as an escape from their problems. Babineau worked in West Berlin as a psychiatrist and documented what he called a "catapulting" phenomenon in which crossing borders, par-ticularly into dangerous or unstable countries, transformed anon-ymous, insignificant people into figures of "central importance and intrigue" who aroused the kind of curiosity and attention that eluded them at home.

"The difficulties begin after they lose their attraction as objects of novelty," he wrote.

Babineau observed that his subjects' need to compulsively cross borders involved idealizing exotic lands while denigrating their home countries, searching for identity, flight from persecution, real or imagined, at home, flight from intimacy, and flight from depression.

Babineau highlighted that "action-oriented persons" sought to remedy their low self-esteem, hopelessness, depression, or feeling of being cornered by traveling to exotic or even dangerous places, where they were at least briefly "catapulted from anonymity, financial or legal distress, into a new situation where they are highly important."

While his research focused on travelers with deep psychological issues, some of his observations may also apply to ordinary compulsive travelers like me and some of the other travelers profiled in this book. Indeed, Paul Theroux touched upon the universality of some of Babineau's themes when he wrote that travel is an "elaborate bumming evasion, allowing us to call attention to ourselves with our conspicuous absence while we intrude on other people's privacy—being actively offensive as fugitive freeloaders."

Traveling to far-off places as "fugitive freeloaders," particularly to the kind of off-the- beaten-path destinations that extreme travelers prefer, makes one an object of curiosity in an appealing way. At home, we can roam the streets for days and few could give a toss who we are. But when you travel, you can reinvent yourself and have a chance to represent your country to people who may have never met someone like you before.

Even a dull person with no striking physical or intellectual attributes can seem unique, appealing, and special when marooned in the Kapingamarangis of the world. Babineau concluded "at the far end of the [traveling] spectrum is a group of restless paranoids, traveling compulsively and seeking by physical flight to be rid of one psychological state and to be catapulted into a newer and better one. Distant reality has a way of looking more malleable than the locally intractable kind." Amen, brother.

❖　❖　❖

The story of the French poet Arthur Rimbaud's escape to Ethiopia in December 1880 is a telling example of a restless soul attempting to alter his psychological state with a dramatic change of scenery. According to a piece in 2015 by Rachel Doyle published in the *New*

York Times, Rimbaud's journey to Harar, Ethiopia, involved crossing the Gulf of Aden on a wooden dhow, followed by twenty days on horseback through the Somali desert.

He was twenty-six but was already in something of a midlife crisis. At nineteen, he wrote "A Season in Hell," a collection of nine evocative poems, in which he penned the memorable line, "I sought voyages, to disperse enchantments that had colonized my mind." The narrator and Rimbaud himself were fixated on roaming. "Outidling the sleepy toad, I have lived everywhere," he wrote. "You don't know where you are going or why you are going, go in everywhere, answer everyone."

A surrealist before there was such a thing, Rimbaud published just one work after his twenty-first birthday. He partied hard in Paris for a time and began a torrid affair with a married man, the poet Paul Verlaine, who, in a drunken rage, shot him in the wrist in a Brussels hotel room in 1873. (Verlaine was initially charged with attempted murder but ultimately served two years for wounding with a firearm. He even suffered the indignity of being subjected to an anal exam, which concluded that he "bears on his person traces of habitual pederasty.")

Rimbaud abandoned his literary aspirations and roamed, often on foot, around Europe, the Middle East, and Africa, sometimes begging in the streets and relying on the police to expel and transport him to a preferred onward destination. According to a biography of the poet written by Graham Robb, Rimbaud "wandered the world for four years without apparent purpose" and was obsessed with learning languages. "This appetite for useful knowledge was beginning to look like a serious addiction," Robb wrote.

He joined the Dutch Colonial Army to get free passage to the Dutch East Indies, and worked as a stone quarry foreman in Cyprus, where he threw a stone, accidentally killing a colleague, before accepting a job with a French trading firm in Ethiopia, then called Abyssinia, at twenty-six. His employer, Alfred Bardey—who clearly hadn't checked the young man's references and probably had no business hiring a surrealist poet in the first place—said that Rimbaud arrived "sick and helpless." Bardey observed that the young writer was "always impatiently waiting for the next occasion to set out on adventures...I could sooner have held on to a shooting star."

According to Doyle's account, Rimbaud rented a thatched-roof home and stayed in Harar for nearly five years—the longest time he ever stayed anywhere as an adult—traveling often to far-flung markets to source coffee and other products for export. Though he bitched about some aspects of his expat life in Ethiopia in letters home, he found a kind of peace there until his health deteriorated.

Suffering from intense pain in his knee that would later be diagnosed as bone cancer, sixteen porters carried him on a stretcher for twelve days to a port in Somaliland in May 1891, where he sailed for France. By the time he arrived, it was too late to save his cancerous leg, which was amputated. Months later, he was pining to return to Africa. That summer, he started the journey south but his health deteriorated and he had to return home, where he was readmitted to a hospital in Marseille. He died later that year at thirty-seven, probably of bone cancer, and Doyle writes that until the end he "was determined to return to the city where he had finally found a kind of peace." His last words were written to the director of a steamship company and refer to plans to take him back to Africa.

Rimbaud referred to himself as an outcast and once wrote, "true life is elsewhere." I don't doubt that he enjoyed his period of exile in Ethiopia but I don't think he found a lasting peace there. The novelty would have burned off if he had been fit enough to return to Africa for good.

Rimbaud's story illustrates that escape artists aren't just hedonists. We also want to experience adversity in a way that we can't at home. The philosopher George Santayana, best remembered for the line, "Those who cannot remember the past are doomed to repeat it," riffed on this in his essay, "The Philosophy of Travel," published posthumously in 1968. "The search for the picturesque is the last and idlest motive of travel," he wrote. "We need sometimes to escape into open solitudes, into aimlessness, into the moral holiday of running some pure hazard, in order to sharpen the edge of life, to taste hardship, and to be compelled to work desperately for a moment at no matter what."

Rimbaud tasted more than his fair share of hardship. But even those with a more stable home life can be seduced by the prospect of the open road, even more so now than in Rimbaud's time. The reality of this era of ubiquitous social media and blogging is that we are hyperaware of the tantalizing possibilities that lurk in terra incognita like goldfish waiting to be swallowed at a fraternity party.

The BBC has a sries called "How I Quit My Job to Travel," and the phrase "travel blog" produces sixteen million results in a Google search. There are thousands, perhaps millions of active travel blogs, and most depict only the sunny side of the traveling lifestyle—welcome to paradise, look at me enjoying this sunset in Bora Bora! And outside the travel genre, books like Timothy Ferriss's mega-bestseller, *4-Hour Workweek*, have encouraged legions of Americans to "escape the 9 –5" and travel the world pursuing one's passions—learn to tango in Argentina!—while working as little as possible.

Many of us can also find inspiration to hit the road simply by scrolling through our Instagram and Facebook feeds, where it seems like there's always someone who is having an adventure somewhere. The selfie stick was invented so people could take "Look-at-me-next-to-" photos. The experience of the traveler has in some ways become secondary to the self-gratifying ritual of boasting about it on social media. But the effect is the same: you see your friend/acquaintance/co-worker seemingly having fun somewhere and you want to go too.

Smartphone technology provides us with more information than we could ever possibly use while ostensibly connecting us to our social circles. But it also reduces our attention spans and may exacerbate restlessness.

The global travel industry has exploded in recent decades, with the number of total international trips skyrocketing from 25 million in 1960 to 536 million in 1995. Since '95, the number of international tourist arrivals has more than doubled to 1.5 billion in 2019.

Restlessness is not new, but we now have more opportunities than ever to indulge our wanderlust. Thanks to the internet, it takes just a matter of seconds to find out that we could live in Bolivia or India or Nepal for a fraction of what it costs to get by in the U.S. And for someone like young William, it would have been easy to find inspiration on the websites of the extreme travel clubs and wonder how he could emulate the travels of some of the world's top travelers.

CHAPTER 12

Today Is Our Day of the Apocalypse

Everything you can imagine is real.

—PABLO PICASSO

Suspicion in some corners of the extreme travel community regarding Baekeland mounted in 2017, as William continued to sporadically postpone some trips while executing others, despite the supposed death of his father in February.

In September, word spread that he had supposedly left Russian travelers who had booked a South Sudan trip with him stranded. His excuse was that he was detained at Heathrow Airport, allegedly due to terrorism concerns inspired by his recent passports stamps from Libya and Syria.

Kolja Spöri, a German national in his forties who lives in Monaco and promotes Formula One and other sporting events, relishes his role as a connector in the extreme travel community. He often wears ascots and a special travel blazer with a myriad of pockets that allows him to travel with little or no baggage. Ranked sixty-fifth on TBT/NomadMania, he started the concept of the Extreme Traveler International Congress (ETIC) in 2008 and in recent years has held these informal shindigs in Chechnya, Gaza, Baghdad, Colombia, and on an ice road in Siberia.

In 2019, the ETIC conference was held in the Principality of Sealand, essentially a platform seven miles off the coast of England. (Unrecognized by any other country, Sealand was founded by the now deceased Paddy Roy Bates, who seized the place from pirate radio broadcasters in 1967.)

The October 2017 event was to be held in Liberland, a micronation with an unrecognized claim to an uninhabited parcel of disputed land on the western bank of the Danube, between Croatia and Serbia. It was proclaimed a sovereign state in 2015 by the Czech libertarian politician Vít Jedlička, who issues passports to like-minded persons who want to become Liberlanders.

The plan was for travelers to convene at the Hotel Leopold I, a grand old dame that's part of an eighteenth-century fortress in Novi Sad, Serbia's second-largest city, on October 20. Spöri had arranged for a number of influential persons in the extreme travel community to make presentations while on board a cruise to Liberland on Jedlička's yacht. William was scheduled to talk about his twelve-thousand-destination Baekelist.

Baekeland had told Spöri that he would be attending along with his mother, Lady Violette, and a friend. According to Mitsidis, William had boasted that by the start of the conference, he would have visited every country in the world twice. When they didn't

Kolja Spöri with Mexican Military

show, travelers compared notes on trips William had cancelled. Many were convinced that the flurry of cancellations and creative excuses was part of a pattern.

Shortly after the ETIC meeting, William cancelled a six-day trip to Timbuktu and other parts of Mali. Harry Mitsidis and three other travelers received an email from a man named David Russell, who identified himself as William's personal assistant, claiming that William was in a hospital and wouldn't be in touch for some time as he needed an unspecified operation. It was unclear whether the hospitalization was connected to the fact that he was allegedly suffering from Crohn's disease. Russell provided no details and when Frenchman Dominique Laurent asked him which hospital he was at, he did not respond.

A number of the travelers were scheduled to leave with William on a (cancelled) trip to Mali in ten days, while others were looking forward to trips Baekeland had planned—and had collected deposits for—to Greenland, Sudan, Somalia, the Democratic Republic of Congo, Antarctica, Saudi Arabia, the epic circumnavigation of the southern oceans, and other far-flung destinations only this group of extreme travelers would want to visit.

Mitsidis spent several days frantically piecing together the pieces of the William Baekeland puzzle and on November 1 sent an email to a collection of about sixty elite travelers with the subject line "Apocalypse Now—A Bomb in Our Travel Community." What follows are excerpts from this message with some names and dates of birth changed for privacy:

> Ladies and gentlemen, dear travellers,
>
> Today is our day of the apocalypse. I am afraid that after reading this message nobody will quite be the same again, and the shock and consternation that I have felt in the last days, as my search has unravelled, will now be shared by all.
>
> So, here is the bomb. William Baekeland does not exist. His whole being and life is the masterful creation of a con artist. The only real thing about William Douglas Baekeland is his middle name.
>
> Jesse Douglas Butcher was born in Sutton Coldfield, a suburb of Birmingham, on March

11th, 1993. His parents are Douglas and Mandy Butcher (nee Vincent). He has two younger sisters, Jessica Grace (born 1996) and Francesca Mary (born 1999). His parents married in 1997 and have lived at 122 Dorchester Road in Birmingham for the past 20-odd years. In the area where they live, average house prices are around 135.000GBP. This is not Knightsbridge by any account, rather a (lower) middle-class area.

Jesse studied international relations at Aberystwyth University, from where he graduated in the spring of 2014. At the same time, starting from 2011 when he was only 18, Jesse was interested in travel and in approaching travellers for an alleged BIOT (British Indian Ocean Territory) expedition. In the period from the autumn of 2011 to the autumn of 2012 I had quite a few email exchanges with Jesse about a possible expedition, as well as trips to Mogadishu and other difficult areas. One of his early victims was Markus Lundgren (a Swedish diplomat) who invested 2500GBP only to never see them again. His attempts to recoup the amount were unfruitful because Jesse had declared bankruptcy. During this period, Jesse formed a company, Remote Worldwide Travel Limited.

In the document dated 7 September 2013
under 'filing history', you can see Jesse Butcher's
birthdate, which matches 'William's' precisely.
One of the amateurish early errors of this conman was registering the company at his home
address, making it all easier to trace.

In the second half of 2014, Jesse presumably
put into action the plan he had already con-
cocted a while before. He would change his
name legally to William Baekeland. The surname choice was, admittedly, a bit of genius,
a name which is not quite world famous but,
if you dig further, is linked to great events
and riches. His plan had already been put
into action as of the autumn of 2013 – I was
contacted by Douglas Baekeland, who then
became an intern for TBT. We had regular
email exchanges and his knowledge of the
world obviously impressed me.

However, late in 2013, Mike Kendall, to whom
we are all incredibly indebted, wrote to TBT
to state that Douglas Baekeland was a conman
whose real name was Jesse Butcher. I was put
in a strange situation, dealing with two people
I had never physically met. As I had Douglas's
CV, I called the school in Switzerland as well as
the Harrodian (a posh school in SW London).
Getting information was not easy but both

confirmed that no Douglas Baekeland ever attended the schools. Faced with this, I decided to drop all contacts with Douglas, and never heard from him again until his grand entrance to the world of travel in March 2015.

You can imagine my surprise, and how shame-faced I felt, when 'William Douglas Baekeland' appeared on the ship to Bouvet, and not only was he on it, he was in an expensive single cabin. Presumably money from his Jesse Butcher scams was used to fund this expedition. This was an incredible ploy, and a fantastic way to build credibility given that nobody had ever heard of him before – apart from me, perhaps. A 35-day trip with way too many days at sea, with more than 60 travellers as possible future victims, all amazed by this young man who was allegedly the heir to a fortune and seemed knowledgeable and polished. 'William' was especially intelligent here, approaching the right people. I now realise how weary he was of me. He knew I had my suspicions.

Fast forward to today. Based on my preliminary investigations, at least half a million euros have been paid in for either trips in the future, or past trips that have been cancelled with bizarre explanations. We never get any information on providers of trips. Some trips are executed, such as my expedition with him to Central African Republic in May, or a trip to Libya in August, but in terms of budget, these are relatively cheap and we don't know how high the mark-up was in the first place.

Meanwhile, future trips have become increasingly expensive. The most hit victim that we are aware of at the moment is [Artem] Tkachev who has given 'William' 166,000 euros. A 70,000[-euro] trip to Greenland which was scheduled for August was cancelled with the explanation that the pilots couldn't get fuel. All requests for information on the company etc. were very politely sidelined, as always. There are at least 10 trips scheduled for the future, of which the Mali and Niger trips have already been cancelled, with no clear word of a refund. I don't know which of the other future trips he planned on actually doing, and which were just scams. I think after this message, anybody willing to still consider travel on any of these is mad.

Ladies and gentlemen, everything you think you know about William is bullshit. You must asked [sic] yourselves what you actually saw with your own eyes — and then admit that you saw what you wanted to see, and fell for it. 'William' was the incarnation of what many of us would have liked to be – young, super-rich, allegedly jetting left and right wherever he wanted. Only that none of his stories were true.

Certainly he incorporated elements of reality – i.e. he does have two sisters, but callously and shamelessly misled people – both his sisters supposedly died in quick succession, one of an illness and the other a suicide, and are buried in Sleepy Hollow. I can imagine that his performance on the Ross island trip this February, during which he supposedly got word that his father died, would put Meryl Streep to shame.

Such fantastic ability to deceive and act, and none of us really asked any questions. So, what exactly have you seen? Has anybody seen his home? His boyfriend? His Irish passport? His alleged heiress mother? Pictures of him as a child? Seen him piloting a plane or boarding a private jet? Met anybody at all who is not from our travel community? The answers are no, no and no.

Because there is no William Baekeland…He also was exceptionally convincing in maintaining an image of a rich boy with relatively small cost but very effective tricks – for example insisting on a $100 upgrade on a domestic flight in Sudan or booking a room in Spitsbergen which would only be used for a few hours and then coming to the airport by taxi rather than the bus.

You may ask how I figured it out. Clearly knowledge of the Jesse Butcher incident helped, but I am most indebted to the country I always trash, the United Kingdom. It is a country where everything is public knowledge, and you can't hide. A few days ago I realised there was no record of a birth of William Baekeland. Everyone else I know who I checked – including myself – had a birth record. Then I checked for Jesse Butcher and, magic, Jesse was born in March 1993. When I then found the company data listed above with the exact same date of birth, it clicked. See, you can't change the date and place of birth on a passport. I am extremely indebted, I say this again, to Mike Kendall. A big thanks also to unassuming Jessica Grace, whose Facebook photos are public for all to see. Little could she imagine that her little note 'my crazy family' would sound so incredibly right to so many world travellers.

His (William's) whole existence has profited not only on our obsessive desire to travel more, but also on our individualism, our lack of cooperation and helpfulness, and how easy it is to criticise. The more isolated and individualist, the more William could approach different people with different offers and convince them to pay for an experience that would give them an edge on others.

So, people, we need to all learn from this... So we need to accept. Accepting that is, of all except the likes of 'William' who has made fools of all of us. Now then. We (yes, it's a we) believe that William could not have acted alone here. He started very young and despite some naïve mistakes, the whole way of behavior and approach was so sophisticated it would be hard for a 21-year old to pull this off (though clearly this was done in a masterful way, so congratulations).

And this is where we give 'William' a small chance. He has exactly 5 hours – until 8 pm UK tonight - to contact me and tell me everything, including who else is involved in this. Maybe 'William' is a victim too, though this will certainly not let him off the hook. No call, and this evening I call the UK Fraud Authorities who will liaise with Interpol as the victims of this that we know of are citizens of Canada, US, France, Germany, Russia and UK (at least, there may be more).

We of course realise that he may try to flee, or change his name again, but given we are talking about a travel addict and someone who likes the finer things in life, there will be no real place to hide – the international police will surely do its job. And if there are more people involved, they will be uncovered, so Jesse – call me and unlike your usual quiet self, you better start talking.

As a community, once again, let's learn our lesson. This awful story should never be repeated. Travel should make us grow, not make us be used and abused.

I also feel I have to write this because we don't know what we are dealing with. I am not suicidal, I am fine and I love life. If ANYTHING happens to myself or my family, you will all know who is responsible. That's all for now.

Sincerely,
Harry Mitsidis

Before the deadline, Tim Wood, William's childhood friend and partner in Atlas Travel and Expeditions, a travel company they formed together in August, responded to Harry on William's behalf. Five days later, Tim sent a more detailed message to a host of travelers who were victims. Excerpts follow:

Dear All Concerned,

I write this email with an extremely heavy heart, and I expect each of you shall receive it with an equally heavy heart. As you all know by now I am William's longtime friend and erstwhile business partner. I intend to continue running the travel company (which had no connection with any of the trips William organised/didn't run) me and William established. I still see, even with the taint of these horrid events, a bright future for it.

So, you all know who I am, in time you will learn that I did not play a knowing part in William's trickery, and can decide whether you ever wish to transact with my company for trips in the future; I will of course understand if none of you do. William's future is uncertain at the moment, and, as we all know, he faces the prospectof [sic] a custodial sentence if convicted in relation [to] this missing money. He will play some role in the planning of trips, albeit he will have no financial control…

I will probably never really understand why he did this, why he took a skill and a viable business organising trips and ruined it for the sake of ego and greed.

When this first came to my attention, and as Kolja Spori suggested to William, my intention was to organise a Skype based 'Meeting of Creditors' to discuss repayments. I see now that this ship has sailed, and that how this is handled is very soon to be out of your hands as well as out of mine, but I wish to state that I am prepared to dialogue with anyone who receives this email.

Once again, it is terribly sad that I find myself writing this email, and terribly sad that you find yourselves, through no fault of your own, reading it. I hope that this debacle will not permanently blight the future of the extreme travel community.

I hope that in years and decades to come this can be looked back on as a real exception to the general rule of honest dealings. It saddens me to think that, in the future, previously trusting travelers may be unwilling to accept offers at face value, or to trust one another with money; this will be William's legacy to a pursuit he was, truthfully, always passionate about, and he'll have to live with the shame of that poisoned legacy for the rest of his life.

Best wishes, Tim Wood.

Mike Kendall, who was an accountant and compliance officer and is a top-one-hundred-ranked traveler on TBT/NomadMania, was suspicious about Jesse Butcher from the beginning and even trolled him on Twitter when he became the jet-setting William Baekeland. But he said in a *Counting Countries* interview that after conferring with Harry Mitsidis and seeing him traveling with a number of top-ranked travelers he changed his mind.

"The more I saw those photos [of William and the elite travelers], then I thought the guy I was trolling was genuine, but I still didn't understand it," he told Ric Gazarian.

Kendall reached out to Baekeland on Facebook and they became Facebook friends. "I didn't say I was sorry but I said, 'I probably owe you a drink,'" he said. Now Kendall wishes he'd stood by his first instincts.

"I don't feel vindicated at all," he said. "I feel bad that many prominent travelers lost money and I didn't shout loud enough."

CHAPTER 13

◇◇◇◇◇◇◇◇◇

Left Behind

Home is so sad. It stays as we left it.

—Philip Larkin

On April 7, 1838, the Victorian-era naturalist Charles Darwin made a list of the pros and cons of marriage. His first line was "If not marry, Travel." And his first point under the heading "Not Marry" was "freedom to go where one liked." (He also fretted that if he married he might become fat, have less money for books, and would waste time visiting relatives, among other concerns.) Darwin was only two years removed from his epic five-year-long journey around the world on board the *HMS Beagle*, an expedition that would later prove pivotal in helping him formulate his theory of evolution.

Despite his reservations, Darwin married Emma Wedgwood, his first cousin, nine months after penning the list. The couple went on to have ten children together, seven of whom survived to adult-hood. Darwin suffered from depression and a host of undiagnosed medical problems throughout his adult life. He traveled here and there during his more than forty years of marriage, but didn't stray too far from Britain for the most part. Married life was probably good for Darwin. Perhaps he needed to settle down in order to make sense of what he experienced in his travels. But did his youth-ful concerns that marriage might inhibit his ability to explore ever resurface? We don't know.

Sir Henry Morton Stanley, a journalist and explorer who was famous for his exploration of Central Africa and his search for the source of the Nile, bonded with the missionary and explorer David Livingstone, when he found him near Lake Tanganyika in 1871, over the costs imposed by their peripatetic lives.

"I have lost a great deal of happiness by these wanderings," Stanley said of his extensive forays across Africa. According to Tim Jeal's book *Explorers of the Nile*, Stanley's nomadic life as a journalist was "a kind of exile [that] had cost him the love of the woman he hoped to marry."

Stanley had met and become smitten with Alice Pike when he was thirty-three and she seventeen, just months before his (second) groundbreaking expedition to Central Africa. Her parents didn't approve of the relationship and Stanley seemed to have a sixth sense that the match was doomed. "I shall fall in love with her, which may not perhaps be very conducive to my happiness, for she is the opposite of my ideal wife," Stanley wrote in his diary, according to Jeal's biography, *Stanley*. Nevertheless, the couple agreed to marry before he departed for what he said would be a two-year journey.

Months later, when Stanley wrote to inform her that his trip might be closer to three years, he received a scathing reply. "And suppose you are not home then, where will you be?" Pike wrote. "Dead or still seeking the Nile?"

Jeal reports that the "crushing" sense of disappointment Stanley felt from Pike's ultimate rejection made the immense fame that followed later seem "hollow and absurd." He channeled his loneliness into a frenzy of writing, producing a 1,092-page two-volume book about his African expedition in just eighty days.

Stanley eventually married late at forty-nine. Paul Theroux neatly summarized the relationship in a *New York Times* review of Jeal's Stanley biography, "She stifled him, refused to allow him to return to Africa, got him to run for Parliament, which he detested, and sent him to exile in an English country house and death at the age of 63."

"I was not sent into the world to be happy," Stanley once wrote. "I was sent for special work."

❖ ❖ ❖

The exploits of noteworthy travelers are well documented, but most reveal little about the people they left behind, the toll extensive travel takes on relationships, and the trade-offs between home life and exploration. Every nomad dreams of having their own faithful Penelope. But in many cases, travelers are lucky to find a mate who will tolerate them being gone for a few months at a time, never mind Odysseus's infamous twenty-year absence.

Laurel Miller, a roving travel writer in her forties who has lived out of a suitcase for years at a time, says that she's single because of her travel compulsion. No man has tolerated her obsession. "Every relationship I've ever had has failed because I love travel more than I have ever loved a guy," she told me in 2015.

Plenty of other travelers have married but found it difficult to stay together. Nina Sedano became a traveler in the wake of a failed marriage. She separated from her husband at twenty-nine, and by thirty-six she calculated that her chance of starting a family was remote.

"Traveling the world was really a plan B for me," she says. "Plan A was to meet Mr. Right and start a family. That never happened so I went off traveling. I don't regret how it worked out."

Our good friend, the "pathological" traveler and dromomaniac Jean-Albert Dadas, met an even more unfortunate fate. According to Ian Hacking's *Mad Travelers*, Dadas found a sweetheart in between traveling fugue binges and got married, apparently after a very hasty courtship. He thought that married life might cure him of his travel compulsion, but before the ink had dried on their marriage certificate, he stole some money from his wife and took off on another fugue, roaming around Europe while his wife wondered where he had buggered off to.

He later told his doctors that he continued to be tormented by a need to travel. Dadas's wife cuckolded him while he was away, and by the time he got back to Bordeaux, months later, she was already married to another man. He eventually remarried, but his wife died of tuberculosis and their only daughter was trafficked into prostitution at age fifteen.

A look at some of the top-ranked travelers on the Most Traveled People website reveals that most are men who are single or divorced. Charles Veley, the founder of MTP, is divorced, and on the *Counting*

Countries podcast interview he was asked about the costs of being one of the world's top travelers.

"Who knows if my marriage would have worked out," he answered, before noting that his traveling lifestyle also left him with less time to spend with his children, who are now fifteen, thirteen, and eleven. Veley, who denied being a dromomaniac, nevertheless said he had no regrets about any of the trips he's taken.

Bob Bonifas has a longtime girlfriend but is also divorced. John Clouse went through six marriages before he died several years ago. Markus Lundgren, a Swedish diplomat who was one of William's very first clients, is one of a very few top country collectors who hits the trifecta: he has a full-time job, a wife, and children. After having twins in 2016, he curtailed his extreme travel habits for a spell. But in 2018, he told me that he was planning a trip to Sudan. "My travel is still limited, but I try to go for a weekend trip every six weeks or so," he explained. He had recently visited Oman and Pakistan alone from his base in Riyadh, and was planning family trips to Bahrain, Kuwait, and Qatar. Lundgren's wife is obviously a sport and a fellow traveler.

Parrish, MTP's number-one traveler and a lifelong bachelor, told me that there's no way he could have visited nearly every spot on the map if he had chosen to have a wife and family.

"I've never had to ask anyone permission to go anywhere," he says. "I just go."

Many others who don't have that luxury struggle to maintain monogamous relationships. "Separation and opportunity test the bonds of love," wrote Elisabeth Eaves in her memoir, *Wanderlust*. "It's more likely that people who hate to make choices, to settle on one thing or another, are attracted to travel. Travel doesn't beget a double life. The appeal of the double life begets travel."

Jean Béliveau, who was away from his partner, Luce, for eleven years while he walked around the world, seemed to be an example of an extreme traveler who had managed to make his relationship work. Luce supported him and his walk, enduring barbs from her friends and relatives, but when he finally returned home, it seemed as though they no longer had anything in common.

Jean Béliveau

"It was awful," Jean admits. "[The reunion] was not romantic at all, as we imagined it would be. It took a year and a half to get close to being back into harmony."

When I first spoke to Jean and Luce in 2012, they had just reentered that harmony phase. But when I spoke to him again in the spring of 2015, shortly after he returned from a walk through Colombia and the Darién Gap, he told me that they were separating. Béliveau said they were on different wavelengths for some time and had finally reached an impasse. He moved to the woods, building a geodesic cabin in a remote area near Danville, Quebec, where he now lives.

Maurizio Giuliano met his wife, an Afghan, in that country just after the Taliban were toppled in 2001. He was working as a humanitarian aid worker stationed in northeastern Congo when I interviewed him in 2015. It was a two-year tour and his wife and two little boys, then ages six and seven, were living in Geneva since it wasn't safe for them to join him. Giuliano gets a few months off each year but says that his family doesn't expect him to spend all that time with them. They know he's a traveler and are accustomed to long absences.

They and others in love with uber-travelers face a choice. Indulge their partner's aspirations to wander and learn to cope with their absences, or object and risk being resented. Partners can always leave if they are fed up, but the children of nomads and extreme travelers have no choice.

Gunther Holtorf is a German man who spent most of a twenty-five-year stretch living with his wife, Christine, in a Mercedes G-Class wagon he calls "Otto" while they traveled to every country on earth, sleeping and eating in the car, avoiding hotels and restaurants all the way. Early on in their travels, they left their son, Martin, then ten, with an aunt, and later he was enrolled in a boarding school so they could continue traveling around the world.

Holtorf says that the experience was good for his son. Their initial trip to Africa, in 1989, was supposed to be an eighteen-month trip.

Gunther Holtorf

"But the more we traveled, the more we realized how little we'd seen," he says, and so they kept going. And Holtorf continued to travel after Christine was stricken with cancer and became too sick to continue because that's what she wanted him to do. Later, Holtorf met a widow, Elke, who became his travel partner, riding shotgun in Otto as they continued to roam the planet, one stop at a time.

There's no easy way for drifters to reconcile their impulse to be free with the demands of family life. The prolific French artist Paul Gauguin was a good provider for his Danish wife, Mette-Sophie Gad, and their children, working as a bookkeeper and then at a bank until January 1882 when the French stock market crashed. According to a biography published in 1937 by Pola, his youngest son whom he abandoned at age two, Mette thought he was "perfectly insane" when he quit his job to focus on his art. Their finances dwindled and Gad got fed up and returned to live with her family in Denmark in 1884. Several months later, he joined them, taking a commission-only job as a tarpaulin salesman.

French tarps didn't exactly sell like hotcakes in Copenhagen and selling tarps obviously wasn't in Gauguin's destiny anyhow. "I hate Denmark with all my heart, its climate and its people," he said after less than a year in the country. In June 1885, he left for Paris, taking only one trunk and his then six-year-old son, Clovis, with him.

In his surprisingly understanding biography, Pola remarked of his father's decision, "[He] had to choose between failing in the duty he felt he owed to his family and being false to himself." Gauguin wrote to his wife some months later telling her she didn't have it so bad. "You enjoy the advantages of marriage without being troubled with a husband. What more do you want, except a little more money?" Clovis, he reported, was taking the move and their penury like a trooper.

"He says nothing, asks for nothing, not even leave to play, and then he goes to bed. This is his life day by day, his heart and his brains are now those of a grown-up person. He is growing fast but is not very well."

Clovis was taken ill with smallpox. As the poor, listless child lay bedridden with a high fever, the hapless painter wrote to his wife that he had just a few coins left and lived on nothing but dry bread for three days. He took a job as a bill poster for an advertising company. After three weeks of laborious toil, with the boy still ill, he was promoted to superintendent with a substantial raise. He told

Mette that he was in line for a big promotion, which would take him to Madrid.

But he quickly changed course, leaving poor Clovis in a pension once he had recovered as he retreated to Brittany to paint. "I miss him very much and if I had had the money, I should have brought him here," he wrote from his new home. "Poor little chap, he won't have any holidays but in this world one can only do what one can." Shortly thereafter, he returned to Paris, and recovered Clovis only to return him to the pension months later. Soon he was buggering off to Martinique, explaining in a letter to his wife, "I can't continue this shattering and enfeebling existence any longer and I'm going to try all I can to have a clear conscience."

He arranged to send Clovis back to Mette, sending her a churlish letter instructing her, "You must find someone who will take charge of him on the journey. I am leaving with just enough for the voyage and I shall arrive in America penniless. What do I expect to do there? I don't yet know myself."

He stayed for only a brief spell in Martinique and saw Mette just once more, in 1891, when he made an unsuccessful attempt to convince her to accompany him to the South Seas. Clovis died at twenty-one of blood poisoning after a hip operation and Gauguin spent the last twenty-three years of his life roaming Europe and the South Pacific, doing exactly as he pleased. Could he have become a groundbreaking artist while being a good husband and father? Perhaps not, but his lonely life of wandering isn't one I'd want to live.

Couples who share the same passion and have the same ability to travel can coexist in harmony. But when imbalances occur, someone has to compromise. The key to success in any relationship is the ability to consider your partner's needs before your own. But asking a hopeless travel addict to stay home is almost like asking them to be someone else. No matter how much you adore your partner, and how terribly you miss them while away, novelty seekers find that the comforts of home can wear off very quickly.

CHAPTER 14

◇◇◇◇◇◇◇◇◇

The Resistance

Life being what it is,
one dreams of revenge.

—Paul Gauguin

In the week after the Baekeland scandal broke, Wood corresponded with a few of the victims and provided some telling details that some believed and others did not. He said that William changed his name in 2014 due to a "falling-out" with his family and maintained that he is indeed a legitimate descendant of Leo Baekeland.

Tim, who said that he had left his job as a wine broker in mid-2015 to work as a kind of assistant to William, attached a photo of his passport and a more recent photo. The passport photo, taken at sixteen, shows a sad-looking, moon-faced teenager with pale skin.

Tim Wood

The recent photo of the twenty-four-year-old did little to establish confidence either. In it, Wood wore a silly-looking barrister robe, he was wearing a pair of dark sunglasses slightly askew, and he was looking away from the camera, like a character in a mob movie.

Dominique Laurent, the retired French financial manager from Paris, was one victim who wasn't buying it.

"William with me chose the very wrong victim," he wrote in one message to Wood. "I [was] not born yesterday! I am 66, worked all my life in international affairs and am a stubborn tough cookie. I will not be afraid to throw money in legal fees. It is a question of honor. I want to make his [William's] life miserable and [make sure] that he gets a strong punishment."

When I spoke to Dominique six months after he lost €50,305, his anger had not abated. He filed a lawsuit against Baekeland in a French court and made police reports with the French police, Garda (the Irish police), and the (UK) National Fraud and Cyber Crime Reporting Center. He even went through ancestry websites to find real descendants of Leo Baekeland and wrote them letters. (Which weren't answered.) I asked him why he considered pursuing Baekeland a matter of honor.

"I gave my confidence to this guy but he fooled me," he said. "He walked on me. There must be some kind of punishment."

Bob Bonifas, who lost $42,000, said that he met with an FBI field agent near Chicago but was told that since he was wiring the money to Irish bank accounts, they would not have jurisdiction over the crimes. He was furious with William and with himself.

"I liked Willliam," he said. "But he's a crook. Once a crook, always a crook. He knows how to scam people. I've been in business for sixty years, and I have never gotten screwed before like this.

These are not dumb people and he got away with it for more than two years. I should have woken up sooner but I didn't."

Like some of the other top travelers, Bonifas had gone on a couple of trips to obscure islands, like Banaba in the Republic of Kiribati, organized by William when he was still Jesse Douglas Butcher with Remote Worldwide Travel Limited. But he and others had never met him in person and had no idea he was the same person when he became William Baekeland in 2015.

While many country collectors wanted to see William's head impaled on a spike, others, including some who lost substantial sums of money, were more zen about their losses. Grosse-Oetringhaus, who lost €74,230, said he had grown close to William and was shocked when the scandal broke.

"You could say he was like a son to me," said the German. "We think we can size people up but William was very clever, very tricky. I never suspected him."

Grosse-Oetringhaus told me he had mixed feelings about the fact that he lost his substantial circumnavigation deposit. He was obviously disturbed by the fact that he, and many others, lost their money. But he also felt a sense of relief.

"It [the circumnavigation] would have been awful," he says. "You expect [that in rough seas] it could be miserable. But as long as it was available, I thought I had to do it. It was available. Now it is not available, so I don't have to do it."

"Why pay a huge amount of money to go on a punishing journey that won't be enjoyable?" I asked.

"We are a different breed," he said. "It's not comfortable but it's interesting, you feel life as it is. It's adrenaline. A kick. It would have been something new and exciting—like going to the moon."

Frank's sentiments neatly distill the essence of wanderlust. It's a powerful force that propels our curiosity and motivates us to enjoy or endure any number of experiences, both positive and negative.

A number of travelers believe that Baekeland's actions were taken to indulge his wanderlust. They don't think he was a professional con man, just a young man who wanted the lifestyle they were leading. One top traveler, who lost a small amount of money with William but traveled with him on several successful trips, called him the "Bernie Madoff" of the extreme travel community. "He's the most successful con man in the travel community ever," he said. "But he also got me to some very difficult places. I don't hate him. I hope he turns around."

Paul Clites is a sixty-five-year-old American who worked in international mergers and acquisitions and is spending his retirement traveling to exotic places around the world. He traveled with William and lost money on Baekeland trips to Timbuktu and the Arctic that never happened.

"People like me and William's other victims, and other avid world travelers who didn't fall victim, must be somewhat eccentric in the base case," he wrote in an email.

"What we do is not 'normal.' Just ask our normal family and friends and they will tell you they don't understand why we don't instead play golf or go to symphonies, or do other normal things."

Clites said that the urge to travel simply infects some people. "We can't *not* do it," he said. "A quote from Diane Arbus summarizes it well—'My favorite thing is to go where I've never been.' But this can lead us to bad decisions for the quest."

The Houston native said that William "had all the symptoms of being travel-infected like the rest of us."

Artemy Lebedev

Other travelers echoed a famous sentiment from Ralph Waldo Emerson, who said, "The truth is beautiful, without doubt; but so are lies." Artemy Lebedev, a Russian entrepreneur who traveled with William on the Northwest Passage, to the Spratlys, Darfur, and on a trip to Rockall Island ultimately lost $60,000 on the circumnavigation trip and another Pacific trip that never happened. He said on the *Counting Countries* podcast that he admired William in a way.

"I really appreciate the greatness of this scam," he said. "It's really great and it's really artistic and I would applaud him for doing all this. He fooled so many people and they are not stupid. I do appreciate even the bad guys." I asked him what he meant and he elaborated via email, "Witnessing such a performance for me is the same kind of joy as watching David Copperfield getting a full-size dinosaur on the scene out of nowhere."

Babis Bizas went a step further on the *Counting Countries* podcast, telling host Ric Gazarian that William was one of two travelers he admired most. And he told me that William should be hired by IBM or another top company.

"To cheat so many people simultaneously, it's a talent," he said. "He cheated high-class people. That means he was smarter than them. It's a talent. I appreciate even the thieves when they do it right."

Baekeland had owed Babis $19,000 for cancelled trips but he badgered him for refunds and ultimately recovered all of his money. He maintains that there is always an element of risk in planning trips and believes that there was nothing wrong with William making a profit for his resourcefulness and hard work planning trips to difficult places.

"They feel humiliated, all the big guys, because they trusted him," he said.

Bizas was at one time ranked number one on both TBT and MTP but left, or, depending on whose version you believe, was removed from these clubs over disputes related to verifying his travel resume. He thinks that the competitive nature of the clubs perverts the true purpose of travel and helped pave the way for William's business.

"The concept of the clubs makes distortion and brings people to the wrong direction," he said. "For those who made the secret trips to Palmyra and Johnston Atoll and others I am not sorry at all for them because they were not clear and open about these trips."

Babis Bizas

Babis, a tour leader who some (including himself) regard as the world's most traveled person, said that William played competitive travelers off of each other, promising to help one gain an advantage over another. And he thinks that what happened could have been prevented, but early victims were reluctant to go public to the rest of the extreme travel community because they didn't want to expose their own secretive travel plans with William. He says they didn't want to be taken off of his invite lists for fear of losing ground to competitors.

"Competition is not good for travel, it leads people to go places, touch the ground, and say they have been there," he said.

Jorge Sánchez agrees. "Traveling is enriching your mind and soul by acquiring knowledge and positive impressions when visiting other cultures and admiring magnificent geographical wonders, not a race to accumulate stupid uninhabited atolls and rocks," he said.

Since he lives in Ireland, David Langan has become the liaison between Garda and William's creditors, even though he isn't owed money. He too thinks that there are lessons to be learned from the Baekeland affair.

"Some of these guys [the victims] all have the same thing in common," he said. "They have too much money, they're comfortable...and there was no competition. It was William or nothing. Their big thing is to travel, and it's more important than their families even. Once they discovered this drug, it [took] over their lives.... Part of it is in me too, but I think I'm able to manage it."

Langan's comments made me wonder about my capacity to manage wanderlust. My travels are limited by time and money but what if I had no such constraints? I too could have been taken in by William.

Pico Iyer summarized the situation well, writing in a Salon.com compendium of travel stories published when William was seven years old, "If travel is notoriously a cradle for false identities, it can also, at its best, be a crucible for truer ones."

CHAPTER 15

◇◇◇◇◇◇◇◇◇

A Fool's Paradise

Tourism is a mortal sin.

—WERNER HERZOG

J ason Lewis spent thirteen years making a 46,505-mile, human-powered circumnavigation of the globe. After completing the expedition in 2007, he made it into the *Guinness Book of World Records* amidst a flurry of media attention. Lewis received a six-figure book-deal offer from HarperCollins, but turned it down because they wanted to use a ghostwriter and he wanted to tell his own story. Less than two months later, he was broke, living in his car in California.

"If you go away for too long, there's really no coming back," he says. "You can't fit back in. In my case, my friends had all moved on, they'd started careers, got married, had kids, and I felt like one of those cartoon characters who falls off a cliff but their legs keep turning."

Jason Lewis

Lewis self-published a superb trilogy of books about his expedition, and is no longer leading a nomadic existence. But the journey changed him, gave him a new perspective on home life. For him, reintegration took years and he's never quite lost his exploring spirit. In 2020, he was planning a zero-carbon circumnavigation of Great Britain before the coronavirus pandemic scuttled his plans.

Others try to settle back into home life and decide it's not going to work. In 1776, after two epic, groundbreaking journeys across the Pacific, Captain Cook was granted a cushy desk job as captain of a medical facility for aging sailors. He was forty-six, with a wife and two boys, ages ten and eleven, and toiled at sea for most of the last decade-plus. He wanted to settle down and become a family man, at least for a time. But according to Tony Horwitz's book *Blue Latitudes*, Cook was miserable within weeks of taking the job.

"My fate drives me from one extreme to another," he wrote to a friend and former employer. "A few [m]onths ago the whole Southern hemisphere was hardly big enough for me and now I am going to be confined within the limits of Greenwich Hospital, which are far too small for an active mind like mine."

Cook conceded it was a "fine retreat and a pretty income," but just a few months later, he came out of his "easy retirement" for what he predicted would be "an [a]ctive, and perhaps [d]angerous [v]oyage." He was searching for the fabled Northwest Passage but ultimately met his end on a beach in Hawaii after being whacked on the head with a club and subsequently stabbed to death.

Few of us suffer a fate that cruel, but nearly all travelers must return home at some point, and the reentry process can be as enjoyable as submitting to a proctologic exam performed by a drunk who flunked out of medical school in Turkmenistan. As the British poet and novelist Philip Larkin wrote, "Home is so sad. It stays as it was left."

Maggie Parker, a freelance writer and self-described travel addict, says that her post-trip depression used to be debilitating. On a trip to Thailand, she felt physically ill on the flight home and then spent a week alone in her apartment upon her return, doing little more than crying and sleeping. She couldn't understand the source of her depression because she loves her job and has a great social life in New York. To search for answers, she wrote a story on travel and depression for Yahoo! News.

"I come down so hard it's as if I'd spent a week on cocaine or ecstasy," she wrote. Parker says she now copes with post-travel depression by planning outings with friends and making sure she has plenty of work to do when she returns from a trip. But when I asked her if those coping mechanisms would help her even if she was unable to travel for a year, there was a long pause.

"No travel for a full year?" she repeated, perhaps hoping she had heard me wrong. "I'm starting to feel sick just thinking about that. No, that would be unbearable."

Parker says that it's a mistake for addicts to immediately seek a new fix when they get home. But that's exactly what many of us do. She admits that she sometimes feels like when she gets that fix, she's just "going through the motions of travel and discovery" to get high again. In other words, the travel itself is secondary to the process.

Steve Bouey is a forty-one-year-old civil servant and ultra-marathon runner in Colorado whose epic three-year, sixty-nine-country journey around the world culminated in his being named National Geographic Co-Explorer of the Year in 2010. He says that his journey around the world was like opening up a Pandora's box. He was happy on the road but suffered bouts of depression when he returned home.

"The best way I can describe it is, I'm homesick for a place I've never been," he explains.

Bouey's biggest regret is the fact that he wasn't "present" for chunks of the trip. Instead of focusing on where he was, he fretted about what was next rather than living in the moment.

Hardcore travelers expend so much energy plotting where to go and what to do that the chase, the pursuit, often trumps the experience itself. Midway through a trip, I start to lose sleep because I'm already dreading going home. I like to have access to my book collection, and I love to enjoy a newspaper, delivered to the doorstep, over a pot of coffee. But those creature comforts quickly lose their novelty, and home starts to feel confining when I have no answer to a fundamental question: Where am I going next?

It's a fundamental drive that's become a part of me I can't suppress no matter what else is going on in my life—health problems, money woes, family obligations, even a global pandemic. I've sometimes wondered if perhaps there was something about my homes that was lacking that made me somehow unappreciative of the so-called comforts of home. But I've lived in all kinds of places, everything from a cockroach-infested, four-hundred-square-foot studio in Brooklyn to a spacious modern (and free) townhouse in Budapest to lovely homes in Virginia and Florida. My drive to travel hasn't wavered, changed, or intensified depending on the quality of my homes.

I'm happiest when I'm living out of a suitcase. I like *not* having a mailbox full of bills and junk mail that I feel compelled to check. It's useful to have my belongings pared down to the bare essentials. For me, familiarity breeds contempt. When I get home from a trip, I often keep my toiletries in their travel case for a spell, just to pretend like the trip isn't over.

My friend Thomas Swick identified "heightened appreciation of home" as one of the seven fundamental joys of travel in his superb book, *The Joys of Travel*. Swick wrote, "The farther you get from home—not just geographically but emotionally—the clearer you see it." I agree with this sentiment but oftentimes this dynamic serves to remind me of things about my home that are lacking. For example, when I was in Australia, I was struck by how drivers would stay to the left and only use the right lane for passing. (They drive on the left, just as in the UK.) I couldn't help but think of the thousand times when I've been stuck behind some stubborn prick in the U.S. going below the speed limit—probably listening to Bryan Adams or playing with their smartphone—in the left lane, refusing to let me pass.

Home should represent comfort, physical and psychological, and it should have a deep significance for me, but it doesn't, and I know I'm not alone on this score. Julie Beck wrote about how the concept of home doesn't have the same significance in Western culture as it does in other societies in a piece on the psychology of home in the *Atlantic* in 2011. "Perceptions of home are consistently colored by factors of economy and choice," she wrote. "The endless options can leave us constantly wondering if there isn't some place with better schools, a better neighborhood, more green space, and on and on."

This is the story of my life, but other travelers feel very differently about their homes. Paul Theroux told me in a 2017 interview that he is happiest when he's in his garden, growing tomatoes. He dislikes hotels and is most productive at home. Don Parrish's favorite place is also his home. That's why he takes his pillow with him everywhere he goes.

Gunther Holtorf always traveled rough—sleeping in his car and cooking all his own meals. He spent most of his traveling life in the developing world and because of this insists that he's never had a hard time going home.

"I realize now how good I have it at home after having seen all the shitty, negative places, all the overpopulated places all around the world," he says. "I'm always glad to be back in Germany where we have space, security, oxygen, and peace."

But does one have to travel in challenging, unpleasant places in order to appreciate the comforts of home?

❖   ❖   ❖

Ralph Waldo Emerson once called travel a "fool's paradise." The nineteenth-century poet, essayist, and lecturer wasn't exactly a stay-at-home type. He made two lengthy trips to Europe, back when this was much more of an ordeal than it is now, in 1832–33 and 1847–8, and traveled cross-country on the transcontinental railroad in 1871, shortly after it was built and while in failing health. Emerson made some valuable observations and contacts on these trips but he thought that travel was overrated, particularly as a means of escaping one's problems:

> The soul is no traveller; the wise man stays at home…. He who travels to be amused, or to get somewhat which he does not carry, travels away from himself, and grows old even in youth among old things…. Travelling is a fool's paradise. At home I dream that at Naples, at Rome, I can be intoxicated with beauty, and lose my sadness. I pack my trunk, embrace my friends, embark on the sea, and at last wake up in Naples, and there beside me is the stern fact, the sad self, unrelenting, identical, that I fled from. I seek the Vatican, and the palaces. I affect to be intoxicated with sights and suggestions, but I am not intoxicated. My giant goes with me wherever I go.

And in a chapter on wealth he wrote in his work, *The Conduct of Life*, at thirty, in 1833, Emerson unloaded on travelers themselves:

> I am not much an advocate for travelling, and I observe that men run away to other countries because they are not good in their own, and run back to their own because they pass for nothing in the new places. For the most part, only the light characters travel.... He that does not fill a place at home, cannot abroad. He only goes there to hide his insignificance in a larger crowd.... What is true anywhere is true everywhere. And let him go where he will, he can only find so much beauty or worth as he carries.

It isn't hard to find travelers eager to evangelize on the benefits of their passion. Skeptics like Emerson may have been more common in the nineteenth century but today it's hard to find anyone with a foul word to say about travel and travelers. Travel haters exist, but many are in the closet. I was limping around the house for the first half of 2015 after suffering a serious knee injury that required surgery. For months, I couldn't even take a walk, let alone a trip. I was miserable, and I started thinking about homebodies and what makes them tick. I wanted to understand how they could be content going nowhere, taking up space on a planet they have little or no interest in exploring.

I read a piece in the *New York Observer* by a travel hater named Lisa Medchill who asserted in 2008 that it was becoming more socially acceptable to admit that she despised travel.

"When I admit that I hate travel, people seem slower to write me off as a listless, incurious slug," she said. Medchill wrote that the week before a trip feels like "imminent death" and said that when she returns home, she feels like a "freed hostage."

Medchill's sentiment hit my eyeballs like a "the world is flat" argument. Was she insane? But I was also intrigued. Medchill called travel a "seedy form of exhibitionism, more something to recount than experience." I'd like to think I'm not one of *those travelers*, but who doesn't know someone who travels primarily for the opportunity to taunt their friends on social media? *Look at me sitting by the pool in Hawaii!*

In the late twenties George Orwell worked for a spell as a *plongeur* (dishwasher) in an upmarket hotel in Paris that he referred to as "Hotel X" in his classic memoir, *Down and Out in Paris and London*. The experience of observing the leisure class enjoying holidays as he toiled through seventeen-and-a-half-hour days in a filthy inferno of a kitchen left him with a cynical view of the tourism industry. He called smart hotels like the one he worked in "enormous treadmills of boredom."

The late writer David Foster Wallace wasn't a bona fide travel hater, but he and Orwell may have been kindred spirits. Foster Wallace's critiques of the tourism industry raised important questions about whether travel benefits the traveler or the people who live in the tourist destination. In an essay on the "nearly lethal comforts of a luxury cruise" for *Harper's*, he revealed how "unbearably sad" the trip made him, admitting that he thought about jumping overboard. (Years later, he committed suicide.)

And on a trip to the Maine Lobsterfest for *Gourmet*, he warned of the detrimental impact of tourism, writing that travelers impose themselves on places that "in all noneconomic ways would be better, realer," without them. Tourists, he wrote, "become economically significant but existentially loathsome, an insect on a dead thing."

Marty Nemko is a travel hater who agrees with Foster Wallace's sentiments. Nemko wrote a piece on his intense dislike of travel for the *Atlantic* in 2012, accompanied by an online poll revealing that *Atlantic* readers preferred "staycations" over vacations by a margin of 2–1. I nearly fell off my seat when I read this. For me, a staycation is almost like a pseudo-experience—a bit like watching a porn movie instead of having sex. I asked Nemko why he and other well-educated, reasonably affluent people would rather stay home.

"I suppose if I had a dull job and lived in a bad climate, I'd want to travel more," he said, "But I live in California and I love my job."

I asked him whether he wasn't curious about the rest of the world, and he said that the more he travels, the less he enjoys it.

"I have a more interesting time in my own office than traveling," he said. "I have interesting clients, I get to write articles, do radio shows, watch and listen to amazing things on YouTube, play with my dog, eat out at places I know are terrific, all without the enormous hassle of traveling. The vaunted benefits of seeing some sights just isn't worth the opportunity cost to me."

Penelope Trunk is a blogger and career coach in Wisconsin who asserts that travel is a waste of time. One of her points—people who love their lives don't leave—felt like a warm bucket of piss tossed in my face. "Imagine if you were excited to get out of bed every day because you had structured your life so that every day was full of what you have always dreamed of doing," she wrote. "And you were in love with your boyfriend, and your job, and your new handstand in yoga. Instead of traveling somewhere, how about figuring out what you'd really love to be doing with your time, and do that in your real, day-to-day life[?]"

Eager to know more about her content-people-stay-home thesis, I called Penelope Trunk and got an earful about why she believes that travel is a self-indulgent waste of time.

"How many people ever found what they were looking for by constant travel?" she asked, before quickly answering her own question. "Travel would be a cheap way to change your life if it worked…but it doesn't. Travel doesn't make you special; it doesn't change you. It's just a way for people to distract themselves by constantly seeking out new things."

Trunk's loathing for travel dates back to her childhood, when her parents, who she says were deeply unhappy people, dragged her on trips around the world, often pulling her out of school for weeks at a time. She became a professional beach volleyball player and then an entrepreneur, and had to travel for her career. Trunk lived in Paris, London, New York, Tel Aviv, and Chicago before moving to a farm in Wisconsin, where she settled down at forty-three, eschewing travel.

Now a career coach, among other things, Trunk says she has read all the research on what makes people happy and insists that frequent travel isn't the ticket.

"Name one successful person who travels for pleasure frequently," she asked, once again posing a question she planned to answer. "Impossible, because there are none. The hardest thing is to commit to a relationship and to commit to being dependable. Being dependable is the opposite of being a traveler. Travel is easy, being reliable is hard."

I couldn't easily dismiss her full-frontal assault on the world of travel—my world, my obsession—but I wanted to know how Trunk and those like her keep their curiosity at bay. "Aren't you curious about other parts of the world? Isn't travel the best way to learn?" I asked. But Trunk insisted that most frequent travelers aren't really out there to learn and grow, but rather to indulge their egos and satisfy their desire to present themselves as worldly and successful.

Annika Ziehen is a travel hater who is a bit different in that she admits that she's an addict, not an abstainer. Here's how she described why she hates travel in a 2016 *Huffington Post* piece:

> Sometimes I wish I would have stayed home. Now I have the daily dilemma of wanting more.... My mind doesn't stand still and quite frankly it is exhausting. I dream of Bangkok when I'm in Cape Town and wish I was in Marrakech, oh no, rather Essaouira when in Florence. I get a plate of Pad Thai and I want Japanese, I find a great Mexican restaurant at home and wish I was back in New York for Venezuelan arepas.
>
> It's not about the grass always being greener elsewhere, I don't care for the grass, but it is about the sky being bluer, the horizon wider, and the smells more exotic.... Always moving, always searching, sometimes arriving, but already planning ahead for the next step which could be just that or a plane ride or a country

away. I am always somewhere, but am I ever here? This traveling business is not for the fainthearted and while I'm not fainthearted, I don't like it very much. However just like my chubby toes and my impatience, it is part of me and I have made peace with it over time. I still hate it, but that is no reason not to love it too.

I can relate to her connection between travel and chronic restlessness. And Trunk's notion that content people tend to stay home makes some sense. But in my case, I love my family and I love my job, so pinpointing the source of my discontent with home life isn't easy. Even though I can't relate to travel haters, I do envy the fact that they can find joy in their day-to-day routine.

But envying someone and wanting to be like them are not the same thing. If I tried to become a stay-at-home type, I'd be haunted by a feeling of missed opportunity—an irrepressible notion that I was missing out on something.

And when I entertain the notion of staying put more often, I think about a month that I spent in the Middle East years ago. I was greeted with unparalleled hospitality everywhere I went. And so, when I hear anyone making breezy generalizations about the Middle East or, even worse, casually advocating for dropping bombs on Iran or other nations in this region, I think about all the people I met and have a very different perspective. Travel can do that for you. But does it make you happy?

Travel is a beautiful escape from reality. There is no finer way to remove oneself from life's dirty, mundane realities than to take a trip. Hate your job? Have a broken heart? Bored with your lot in life? Step right up and book a ticket to just about anywhere. The trip might change your life—or maybe it won't.

The travel industry promotes the idea that a vacation will make us happier and that our trips will be *life-changing*. The term "life-changing travel" generates 984,000 results in a Google search. *Travel + Leisure* suggests twenty "Life-Changing Trips." CNN Travel has forty-nine "Journeys That'll Change Your Life." NBC News details a list of "Incredible Trips *Guaranteed* to Change Your Life." *Coastal Living* offers a list of "11 Vacations That Will Change Your Life," with a suggestion to "add these amazing experiences to your travel bucket list," using the assumption that travelers may need to change their lives on multiple occasions. Sadly, *Coastal Living* doesn't explain how learning to surf in Costa Rica, taking a cooking class on the Amalfi Coast, or any of its other pedestrian suggestions would change someone's life.

Even Martha Stewart has gotten in on the act with "Ten Life-Changing Travel Rules," among them "assemble outfits in advance," "make sure chargers don't get tangled," and "fold properly to avoid wrinkles."

Hundreds, perhaps thousands, of tour companies market quotidian trips as life-changers.

G Adventures, for example, features a page on its website titled "We Love Changing People's Lives" with a page of testimonials from clients whose lives were "transformed" after taking one of their trips:

> At G Adventures, changing people's lives isn't
> just a mantra, it's the very core of our company
> culture, the essence of who we are, and the
> driving force behind everything we do.

Aggressively marketing trips as "life-changing" makes good business sense. So many of us find modern life—the routine of office work, evening TV, the distraction of social media, and the insipid consumption of internet listicles ("Top Ten Painful Illnesses!")—uninspiring and, at times, meaningless. We're easy marks because we want very much to believe that a trip can bring meaning to our lives.

According to the World Travel & Tourism Council, one of every eleven adults on the planet is employed in the travel industry. The U.S. Travel Association estimates that the domestic travel industry generated $2.6 trillion in economic output in 2019. This means there is a massive stake in promoting tourism as a shortcut to happiness, a new life, or both. Just look at almost any travel blog—the message is almost always the same: this is the good life. Come get it.

In light of the stakes, any hint that a person's travel compulsion, taken to an extreme, might have a detrimental impact on their marriage or career or mental health is taboo. Travel writers are effectively bribed with free trips and upgrades, and can typically be counted on to churn out the kind of this-place-is-paradise pieces that editors and advertisers demand. They rarely write about the bad trips or the toll that their traveling lifestyle takes on their families or the loneliness that often goes with the territory when one is away from home for extended spells.

The travel media is unlike any other genre of writing in this way. Imagine a world in which there were no bad film, restaurants, theater, music, or book reviews. The cumulative effect of all this feel-good travel writing is that it's very easy to be seduced into thinking that there is no such thing as a bad trip.

But while very few of us dwell on what went wrong on the road, many compulsive travelers admit that coming home can be rough, especially for those who return to confront seemingly intractable problems. While many of us afflicted with the nomadic curse are pursuing happiness—sometimes to the ends of the earth—some of us suffer from the delusion that we might find it if we keep on traveling.

There's been very little, if any, research on the impact of leisure travel on relationships, careers, or mental health. But a 2018 study conducted by Columbia University's Mailman School of Public Health "found a strong correlation between the frequency of business travel and a wide range of physical and behavioral health risks."

Compared to those who spent one to six nights a month away from home for business travel, those who spent fourteen or more nights away from home per month had significantly higher body mass index scores and were significantly more likely to report the following: poor health, anxiety, depression, alcohol dependence, smoking, and trouble sleeping. The authors of the study also cited a study of health insurance claims among World Bank staff and consultants, which concluded that travelers had significantly higher claims than their non-traveling peers for all conditions considered, including chronic diseases such as asthma, back disorders, and stress disorders.

Business travel is obviously a different kettle of fish than leisure travel. But compulsive travelers tend to avoid posh resorts in favor of difficult, stressful destinations in developing countries. Travel in

South Sudan or the Central African Republic is not really a holiday. And, no matter where you go, if your family isn't with you, ties can become strained the longer you're away from home, regardless of the purpose of your travel.

Dr. Gianna Moscardo is a professor at James Cook University in Australia who studies travelers in order to better understand the correlation between travel and quality of life. She says that this field of study doesn't get much respect in academia. Moscardo believes that many tourism researchers highlight, and in some cases over-state, the impact of travel as a life-changing event ("It's not just fun in the sun! It's life-changing!") in order to be taken seriously.

And Moscardo says that what she calls "survivor bias"— the reality that it is much easier to find people who boast of the life-changing nature of their travels than those who were disappointed or even troubled by their experience—can explain some of this exaggeration.

"I found that people who didn't travel or had traveled once and didn't like it were often vilified for being narrow-minded, inflexible, or cowardly," she says. "Travel is such a marker of modern life it is difficult for someone to openly admit that it [sometimes] just isn't that great."

Moscardo believes that many travelers also like to boast that their journeys were "life- changing" to justify the expense and time spent on travel. She says that we also spin bad trips, citing a recent experience where she was robbed in Belgium.

"I found myself telling someone, 'Well, it was a negative experience, but I feel like I learned about my own resilience and ability to cope and I'm a better person for it,'" she recalls. "But even as I said it, there was this other voice saying, 'Bullshit—it was horrible.'

I think the second voice might be closer to the truth, but I'm still using the first voice when I get asked about it."

In a paper on the connection between travel and quality of life, Moscardo raises the possibility that travel is an "egocentric, status-driven activity, generated in part from the failure of individual tourists to find meaning in their daily lives, with only temporary benefits at best."

And in a 2018 study she co-authored that studied how tourism impacted the quality of life of locals in three Australian locales, Moscardo and her colleagues concluded that "a higher scale of tourism development was linked to increased crime, reduced volunteering and perceived influence over community development." They also observed that locals in the communities they studied "did not demonstrate a higher emotional connection to place, community pride, and needs fulfillment that are commonly assigned to benefits of tourism development."

Dr. Jeroen Nawijn is a lecturer at NHTV Breda University in the Netherlands who has studied the correlation between travel and happiness. In 2010, he published a paper based on a study of 1,530 Dutch adults, 974 of whom took a vacation during an eight-month period. Dr. Nawijn concluded that while people felt happier planning trips and also during their holidays, their happiness bump often disappeared when they returned home.

In a 2017 study, "Between Tourists: Tourism and Happiness," Nawijn and his colleagues attempted to determine if those who traveled for a longer duration or for shorter, more frequent trips derived more happiness. They concluded that length and frequency of travel did not impact subjective well-being. "While holidays generally improve positive emotions during a tourism experience, and tourism events and circumstances may affect well-being, how long and how often individuals travel for holidays over the course of a single year does not affect their well-being in the months that follow."

A 2015 study, "A Darker Side of Hypermobility," authored by Scott Cohen and Stefan Gössling, researchers from the University of Surrey and Lund University in Sweden, asserted that while travel is glamorized, there was an "ominous silence" with respect to the "darker side" of the hypermobile lifestyle.

"The level of physiological, physical and societal stress that frequent travels [place] upon individuals has potentially serious and long-term negative effects that range from the breaking down of family relationships, to changes in our genes due to lack of sleep," the authors wrote. "Social media encourages competition between travellers to 'check-in' and share content from far-flung destinations. The reality is that most people who are required to engage in frequent travel suffer high levels of stress, loneliness and long-term health problems.... By striving to travel far, wide and frequently we are damaging the environment, ourselves and potentially our closest loved ones."

❖   ❖   ❖

While there doesn't seem to be much empirical evidence that trips make people happier long- term, it's hard to deny that there is often a very short-term boost. Researchers from the University of Vermont who examined some four million tweets in 2013 concluded that the farther from home someone is, the happier they are. By this token, chronic travelers should be the happiest people in the world, provided they stay far away from home. But are we?

Quite a few of the world's most obsessive travelers and explorers have been deeply unhappy people who were restless because they were dissatisfied with their lives in some fundamental way. In his engaging book *Explorers of the Nile: The Triumph and Tragedy of a Great Victorian Adventure*, Tim Jeal surmised that the notable explorer Sir Richard Burton's "dissatisfaction with himself...was only appeased by visiting wild places." He described his wanderlust as a "mania for discovery."

An unabashed imperialist and impish connoisseur of hookers who believed that the Americas and most of Asia were hotbeds of pederasty, Burton was one of the first non-Muslim Europeans to make the hajj to Mecca in 1853. He dressed in disguise as a peddler of potions and horoscopes and even had himself circumcised before the journey to ensure he could pull off the feat. Burton avidly chronicled his travels in exotic places, describing local cultures, sexual mores, and even the respective penis sizes of men in various places. (Apparently he traveled with rulers in his carry-on luggage.)

Burton was guided by curiosity, but he understood that exploration wasn't an effective tonic. His father, an asthmatic retired colonel, dragged the family across the continent, moving from place to place many times in his childhood in a vain attempt to find a place where he could regain his health. Burton famously remarked, "Men who go looking for the source of a river are merely looking for the source of something missing in themselves, and never finding it."

Francesco Petrarch, a fourteenth-century Italian poet and scholar who is considered one of the fathers of the Renaissance, understood this centuries ago. Petrarch is reputed to be the world's first tourist, but he came to question the utility of leisure travel after climbing to the top of Mont Ventoux on April 26, 1336. While admiring the French alpine scenery, he pulled out a copy of St. Augustine's *Confessions* and was shocked by words that seemed to be a blunt rebuke of his lifestyle.

"And men go to admire the high mountains, the vast floods of the sea, the huge streams of the rivers, the circumference of the ocean and the revolutions of the stars—and desert themselves."

Petrarch reportedly retreated from the pursuit of natural beauty into the inner world of spirituality. He died of the plague in 1361, at seventy, though we don't know if he gave up on travel entirely or whether he still enjoyed sneaking off to Interlaken for a weekend of hang gliding and zip-lining, just for shits and giggles.

Paul Theroux, no travel hater by a long shot, riffed on how some of modern history's great travelers were deeply troubled in his excellent book *The Tao of Travel*. He detailed how David Livingstone, Sir Richard Burton, Jack London, Graham Greene, Captain Robert Scott, and others were "depressives or bipolar types capable of serious gloom," but didn't speculate as to why so many noted travelers suffered from depression. Nevertheless, I had a chance to ask him about the trend in a June 2017 telephone interview.

"Wanderlust is a search for happiness," he said. "It's a quest for something you don't have. So many travelers have been depressives. People who travel go for a reason; it's a search. If a traveler decides to stay in one place, he's happy. If they move on, it's because they haven't found what they're looking for. The whole nature of travel is like a search for something better."

Theroux also suggested that there was an element of "misanthropy" in wanderlust. "In many cases, you're not traveling to meet people, you're going to escape *from* people," he said.

Theroux's list of noteworthy depressed travelers in *The Tao of Travel* only scratched the surface of a remarkable trend. Peripatetic Jack Kerouac, author of *On the Road*, the book that inspired millions of young people to travel, suffered from bouts of depression. So did Ian Frazier, another writer who has spent much of his adult life on the road and once wrote, "My only opportunity for an old-fashioned, self-indulgent sulk comes when I'm traveling."

Scores of other peripatetic writers have also struggled with depression, including Hans Christian Andersen, F. Scott Fitzgerald, Mark Twain, James Joyce, Ernest Hemingway, Hunter S. Thompson, Bruce Chatwin, Ryszard Kapuściński, V. S. Naipaul, Arthur Rimbaud, Samuel Beckett, Fyodor Dostoevsky, Joseph Conrad, William Faulkner, Henry James, Agatha Christie, and others. So, too, did restless artists and explorers like Johnny Cash, Alexis de Tocqueville, Captain James Cook, Sir Edmund Hillary, Paul Gauguin, Georgia O'Keeffe, Jackson Pollock, and Vincent van Gogh, who lived in twenty different cities and once said, "I am not an adventurer by choice but by fate."

And a slew of other celebrated explorers and travelers were manic-depressives, including Christopher Columbus, Meriwether Lewis, Charles Darwin, Edgar Allen Poe, and Charles Dickens.

Several of the most acclaimed travel narratives in print are accounts of journeys that were inspired by illness, mourning, or depression. John Steinbeck made the road trip that became *Travels with Charley* because he knew he was dying and wanted to see the country one last time. (Though some have accused him of mixing fact and fiction in his account of this trip.) The loss of his job and his wife inspired William Least Heat-Moon to make the cross-country pilgrimage he described in the bestseller *Blue Highways*. Paul

Theroux was in a funk after a health scare and the dissipation of his marriage when he paddled the Pacific and wrote *The Happy Isles of Oceania*.

Geoffrey Moorhouse's *The Fearful Void* is about a trek across the Sahara by camel, taken in the aftermath of his failed marriage. (The book was a bestseller, but both of his next two marriages also ended in divorce.) And Peter Matthiessen was mourning the loss of his wife when he took off on the Himalayan adventure described in his classic book *Snow Leopard*.

It would be wrong to argue that these people were unhappy because they traveled. They were restless because they were searching for something—a refuge, an escape, novelty, love, happiness. And thanks to their occupations, they weren't confined to an office, so they were freer than most to go looking. As Hemingway once said, "A writer is an outlier, like a gypsy."

As the Twitter study concluded, many of us feel a happiness boost when we travel. Frank Wigand Grosse-Oetringhaus says his yearning for travel (the Germans call it "*fernweh*") is the opposite of homesickness. "I love the world and the more I see of it, the happier I am," he says.

Maurizio Giuliano, the Italian globe-trotter, agrees, saying that he cannot "disassociate" travel and happiness.

"I don't understand why some people want to stay at home," he says. "It's like trying to understand people who are asexual. I will never understand people who have no passion for traveling. I may have an addiction to crossing borders. I have a special feeling when I cross a border and when I'm in a different country."

I can relate. But one of the risks of compulsive travel is that we can become jaded. George Orwell, a restless type who lived in England, Scotland, France, Spain, India, and Burma and who worked in a hotel in Paris, chronicling the experience in his memoir, *Down and Out in Paris and London*, once called smart hotels "enormous treadmills of boredom." Perhaps, but only for those who have been to quite a few in various parts of the world.

If we believe that we need to travel in order to be content—when our idealized version of bliss is riding an elephant in Africa or climbing Mount Kilimanjaro—it's difficult to adapt to home life and appreciate life's everyday pleasures like greeting our kids at the bus stop or savoring an ice cream cone. In many ways, the happiness bar climbs with every trip we take.

The question of whether travel increases long-term happiness is unresolved. But it's worth noting that the Harvard Study of Adult Development, the world's longest-running study on happiness and what makes a good life at nearly eighty years (and counting) emphasizes that close relationships are the key to happiness and good health.

Scientists at Harvard began to track 268 Harvard sophomores, including the future president, John F. Kennedy, to gain insights into what made for a healthy and happy life. Less than twenty of these men are still alive, but the study has also tracked their descendants, along with hundreds of inner-city residents who were added to the study in the 1970s.

The key finding of the study is that "[c]lose relationships, more than money or fame, are what keep people happy throughout their lives. Those ties protect people from life's discontents, help to delay mental and physical decline, and are better predictors of long and happy lives than social class, IQ, or even genes." Their findings were consistent for both the Harvard men and the inner-city residents.

The operative question with respect to wanderlust is how travel impacts our key relationships. If a person's travel addiction alienates them from their spouse, children, or close friends, then it won't bring them happiness or health. But if travel brings them closer to those people, then it could.

Ernest Hemingway once said, "Never go on trips with anyone you do not love." And Mark Twain said, "[T]here ain't no surer way to find out whether you like people or hate them than to travel with them."

In our case, I believe our extensive family travels have brought us closer together and have brought us a lot of happy times. But the trips always come to an end. And when one has to be away to feel joy, home life can taste a lot like a non-alcoholic beer—essentially just a substitute for what you really want.

And the prospect of returning to "normal" life can be daunting. I met Gilly Snaith and her husband Steve, a British couple who drove nearly 180,000 kilometers to fifty-eight countries on all seven continents while "worldschooling" their daughters, Lucy and Alisha, when I was traveling in Belize in 2015. We stayed in touch and I was fascinated by their epic family journey.

Eight weeks prior to the end of their five-year drive around the world, the traveling Snaith family feared what would come next.

"Sadly the end of our trip is in 8 short weeks," Gilly Snaith wrote in June 2017. "'Normal' life is scarily looming close on the horizon. I am sure the readjustment will be one of the biggest challenges of the trip. Especially for Steve and I, as we haven't lived in the UK for over 20 years now. The girls are looking forward to being close to relatives and to going to school—[but] I'm not sure how long that will last."

Another worldschooling family I met in Peru had a similarly difficult transition back to sedentary life. The Tupy family completed their ten-thousand-plus-mile road trip from Cusco to Niagara Falls in their psychedelically painted VW Kombi bus in June 2017, about two years after they set off. The Kombi broke down in nearly every country they visited, and they stopped to work and crowdfund along the way to pay for repairs and visas and such. They settled in Moncton, New Brunswick, a new place for them where they knew no one.

"There was no real forethought," Michelle Tupy said in a January 2018 email. "We kind of just stopped the trip and found an apartment where our trip ended."

Tupy said that the reality of staying put with the kids in a local school—and enduring their first real winter in four years—was extremely challenging. "While it is nice to have a base, I have moments of sadness, anger and depression regarding the fact that we don't have as much freedom as we did," she said. Making matters more difficult, she was applying for Canadian citizenship and couldn't leave the country even if she wanted to until her application was processed.

Still, Tupy said that her moments of anger and depression were usually fleeting. She was buckling down, working on a book, staying positive, and, most importantly, staying busy. "While we are not indulging wanderlust directly, we are looking at other avenues where we can direct our wandering minds," she said.

❖   ❖   ❖

Nearly four hundred years ago, the French philosopher Blaise Pascal said, "I have discovered that all of the unhappiness of men arises from one single fact—that they cannot sit quietly in their own chamber." He argued that people naturally seek "turmoil" but said, "Their error does not lie in seeking excitement, if they seek it only as a diversion; the evil is that they seek it as if the possession of the objects of their quest would make them really happy."

Pascal's remarks are more relevant now than ever in a world where many of us are about as patient as a man in the middle of robbing a bank. According to a recent study conducted by psychologists at the University of Virginia, two-thirds of men and a quarter of women chose to give themselves mild electric shocks in order to avoid having to sit in a room alone, doing nothing.

I'm the kind of hyperactive person who views idleness as a punishment. When I'm left alone to my own thoughts, I worry about our finances, my career trajectory, my health. Even when I'm out for a walk or a bike ride, or when I'm lying down in bed, I'm always listening to a book or a radio program, in part because I don't like retreating too deeply into my own head.

That said, when I heard globe-trotting travel writer Pico Iyer had a book out called *The Art of Stillness*, I was intrigued. How could a kindred spirit like Pico advocate going nowhere? I read the book and listened to a talk he gave, hoping I might learn something that would make me feel better about staying home during a time when I was too ill to travel. Iyer argued that going nowhere is a "grand adventure" that helps one make sense of everywhere else they've been.

"I found that the best way that I could develop more-attentive and more-appreciative eyes was, oddly, by going nowhere, just by sitting still," Iyer wrote. "To my great surprise, I found that going nowhere was at least as exciting as going to Tibet or to Cuba."

As Iyer's meditations percolated around my brain on an unseasonably warm winter day in Bend in late 2016, I got an email from Jorge Sánchez, the Barcelona man who has traveled the world on a shoestring. Jorge recently returned from a round-the-world trip and was unemployed.

"I am surviving with a maximum of 10 euro a day in food and other small expenses, and I am afraid that within a few months I will have to reduce that amount to 5 euro per day," he wrote. "So that is my real situation. No money means no travels. It is the end of my journeys; force majeure."

Sánchez said that he had met a woman in Russia who was pregnant with his child and he didn't want to lose his new family.

"Most people travel 1 month every year during their holidays, and when they become pensioners, they travel very intensively (see Don Parrish and many others). My life has been the opposite, I only traveled when I was young, that is 30 years of my life net on the road, and now that I am 61 I have no more money and no way to earn it. It is like in the fable of the grasshopper (who spent the winter months singing) and the ant (who worked to store food for the winter.) I am the grasshopper. I do not regret anything, I am happy with the life that I have chosen, so now I have to face the consequences."

His comments reminded me of some advice Frank Grosse-Oetringhaus had given me:

> Your contentment should come from the awareness that you prepare yourself for the ability to travel. You cannot have everything right away. Now you are preparing [to travel] and the prospects are making you happy, you

have a dream, a goal that you are living for....
Before retirement the source of your happiness
should not come out of traveling, because it
only can be limited. And the limitation should
not make you unhappy, because your happiness
comes from a professional career, from family
life, and a working life that could be directed
to helping other people. Traveling in this phase
has to take a pragmatic point of view; you do
what you can do. But you don't expect more.

It was good advice, but it fell into the "easier said than done"
category for me. In spirit and mentality, I'm closer to the passionate
Spaniard than the pragmatic German.

I wrote back to Jorge, asking him whether he wasn't depressed to
be grounded at home, pinching Euros in Barcelona. He responded
immediately.

"I do not know what is depression," he wrote. "I enjoy life no
matter what I am doing, at home or on the road. Living is a miracle.
I never forget that. Life is superior."

When I first spoke to Jorge, months before, he said he had chosen a life of travel over family and insisted that a lack of money had
never kept him grounded. Now he had found someone who had
changed his priorities. In a way, I was a little disappointed. I wanted
him to say, "You're right, being at home is a kind of torture!"

The more I thought about his sentiments, however, it dawned
on me that it is very easy to take the people you love for granted,
and to obsess over what makes *you* happy. But it's a true labor of
love to put your desires on the back burner and focus on making
the people you love happy.

Gilly Snaith and her husband, Steve, returned to England in August 2017 because they wanted their girls to have a chance to put down roots and be near family. I admired their willingness to prioritize what they perceived to be their daughters' best interests over their own desire to keep traveling. But on their blog, Gilly admitted that coming home was rough.

"Even after all these weeks it still seems very peculiar to pull back the curtains every morning and see the same view," she wrote. "The girls have adapted very quickly to their new life but Steve and I still feel the strong pull of the open road."

Facing the problem of home squarely in the face, they did just what I would have. "As the British winter weather moves in our thoughts turn again to new adventures, although shorter ones to fit in with the school holidays," she wrote. "We've just booked the truck onto the ferry to the Faroe Islands and Iceland for next summer."

CHAPTER 16

◇◇◇◇◇◇◇◇

Chasing Mr. Baekeland

*The ideal travel book should be perhaps a little like a
crime story in which you're in search of something.*

—CHRISTOPHER ISHERWOOD

Lurking in my car outside the home of whom I believed to be a legitimate Leo Baekeland descendant, I felt like a stalker. A neighbor emerged from her home with a dog on a leash and caught my eye. I looked down at my phone hoping she'd leave and she did. Dominique Laurent had given me the names of the Baekeland heirs he'd written to. None had much of an online footprint, but I noticed that one lived in Portland, which is three hours away from my home in Bend.

I couldn't find her phone number online but I was scheduled to go to Portland for a doctor's appointment in April 2017, so there I was on a lovely spring day, sitting in front of a smart but far from opulent home on a quiet, tree-lined street very close to Portland's Japanese Garden. I was hoping to find out more about the Baekeland family and perhaps come to understand why William had chosen to take their surname.

I had no idea if Mr. Laurent's research was accurate or if my target still lived at the home, but I approached the front door with trepidation, clutching a letter of explanation I planned to leave if no one answered. I rang the doorbell and saw out of the corner of my eye that there was a security camera mounted above me to my left. My heart thumped as I rehearsed what I was about to say if someone answered the door. I hoped that in a city whose unofficial motto is "Keep Portland Weird" my "I'm writing a book about wanderlust" speech wouldn't immediately prompt a call to the police.

I waited a minute or two, and when no one answered, felt a bit relieved to leave my letter under the mat and hightail it out of the neighborhood. A couple days later, I was back in Bend and I got an email from the owner of the home where I'd left the note. He said that the person I was looking for—I'm going to call her Joanne (I'm withholding her real name to protect her privacy)—had moved and he gave me her new contact information.

Later that week, I spoke to Joanne, who is a fifth-generation descendant of Leo, on the phone. She had received Dominique's letter and knew all about William's story. The Baekeland family, she said, felt guarded and a little burned after the book and film *Savage Grace*, which portrayed members of the family as rich, idle jet-setters who were essentially pissing away their inheritances.

Joanne said that she and other members of the family decided not to respond to Mr. Laurent's letter because they were leery of what he and other victims might want from them. She said that the

Baekeland heirs were shocked that William was leading people to believe he was a wealthy heir to Leo's fortune.

"If you compare the lifestyle he was purporting to have compared to our actual generation, we are not living that lifestyle," she said. "We all work. We all have jobs. We are not living off of family money. It's a big disconnect from reality. I was really surprised. We are living normal middle-class lives."

Joanne told me a bit about Leo and directed me to a relative who made a film about him, *All Things Bakelite*. Leo was born in Belgium to a family of modest means—his mother was a maid and his illiterate father repaired shoes—and emigrated to the U.S. in 1889. A photography buff, he went to work for a photographic supply manufacturer and then invented Velox, a photographic printing paper that didn't require natural light for development.

Leo made a fortune in 1899 when Kodak paid him somewhere between $750,000 and $1 million (something like $20–$28 million in 2020 dollars). In 1907, while experimenting to find a substitute for shellac, Baekeland invented what he called Bakelite, an inexpensive, nonflammable, and versatile plastic.

Bakelite became the material of choice for a huge array of manufactured products, and Baekeland ultimately sold his company to Union Carbide for $16.5 million in 1939. He died in Beacon, New York, in 1944, at the age of eighty, and was buried in Sleepy Hollow Cemetery in Tarrytown, where William claimed his two sisters (who are very much alive, according to Harry Mitsidis) were laid to rest.

Joanne said that despite his wealth, Leo was very frugal.

"There are stories that he liked to heat up a can of soup on a Bunsen burner and that was his dinner," she said. "All he wanted to do was sit in his room and invent things."

Leo retired to a simple house in Coconut Grove, Florida, and established a trust that allowed some of his descendants to live comfortably. But, according to Joanne, the money that's flowed to the current generation of Baekelands is relatively modest.

"'Billionaire' is a big overstatement from what I know," she said.

Interestingly enough, Leo was also a traveler. According to the timeline put together by Hugh Karraker, the family historian who made the film about Leo, in the summer of 1906 Leo shipped his Peerless limousine to Southampton for a tour of Great Britain, France, and Italy with his family. He later wrote a book about the adventure, *A Family Motor Tour through Europe*, which was published by an automobile trade magazine.

In one section of the book, Leo published a thoughtful mediation on the perils of wanderlust:

> Most of the time people who travel try to cajole themselves into the belief that they are enjoying themselves, while in reality they are merely spending money right and left in increasing amounts without great satisfaction, or they keep rushing from one country to another in vain search of happiness. I have known such people who from the mere fact of being in a certain city were overcome by ennui, which caused them to move to another place, where their implacable tormentor, ennui, followed them as fast as any train or automobile could carry them.

❖   ❖   ❖

With William seemingly in hiding, I tried calling Wood shortly after my Portland trip and was surprised that he answered. He said that William was reclusive and had no interest in "setting the record straight." Wood, who said he has a law degree but doesn't practice, described William as a person with an "IQ off the charts" who could "charm the birds out of the trees." He said that he had some sympathy for the creditors, but said that they were partly to blame for the situation as they all demanded refunds at the same time, causing a "run on the bank" situation that left William's fledgling company short of funds.

I pressed him regarding the name change and he insisted that William was indeed a great-grandson of Leo Baekeland, contrary to the Baekeland family's claims.

"It's not all untrue," Wood said of William's backstory. "They have put a sinister gloss over it. He does have noble lineage—he has an aristocratic background."

Wood told me that a number of travelers had maligned William by claiming that he was working class and telling other lies about him. He said that Baekeland had initiated defamation suits in the U.S. and the U.K. against some travelers (he wouldn't say who).

"He may have to pay them $50,000 back but then they'll owe him $1 million for defamation," he said before elaborating that UK libel laws place the burden of proof on the defendant rather than the plaintiff.

Wood rambled about William's Scottish clan, the Marquess of Huntly, baronies, and such and I tried to focus back on motive. Why did he do it? Was he seeking a way to fund his own wanderlust, I asked, or was he just a con man?

"If he had wanted to be a con man, he could have made any amount of money, tens or hundreds of millions in art or investment or wherever, he wouldn't have chosen travel," he said. "He could have done it properly and made much more."

Wood brought up the term "dromomaniac" and said it did indeed apply to William. "He had this list of twelve thousand places, he really did have it on a spreadsheet on his computer," he said. "You couldn't fake that. He is still a traveler and he always will be no matter what happens."

KINGSTANDING: A PLACE KNOWN FOR NOTHING AT ALL

Driving three miles north of William's childhood home on a blistering hot Monday morning in late July 2018, I started to believe that perhaps Wood was right to insist that William's roots weren't as working class as advertised. While in Europe with my wife and boys, I was determined to look into the Baekeland story where it all started. I set off alone in a fancy hired Mercedes Benz from our rental cottage in England's Peak District with an address on Dormington Road, north of Birmingham, programmed in my GPS.

The Baekeland affair hit the press in May 2018, first on the website of *Rolling Stone* and later in the British tabloids. An article in the British newspaper *Daily Mail* asserted that William had lived with his parents in a £130,000 ex-council house (council houses are akin to public housing in the U.S.) next to a bingo hall. Harry Mitsidis wrote in his apocalypse email that it was a "lower middle class area," commenting, "This is not Knightsbridge by any account."

But just minutes from my destination, I was motoring along Rosemary Hill Road through a privileged landscape of stately homes partially hidden behind tall, immaculately trimmed hedges, posh golf clubs, and fit women pushing expensive-looking strollers. I wondered if perhaps Baekeland's purported humble origins had been exaggerated to create a Horatio Alger, rags-to-riches element to his story. In the space of a mile or so, though, the picture changed dramatically as I motored south into a decidedly gloomy, working-class neighborhood I learned was called Kingstanding.

I parked the car near a massive roundabout that appeared to be the neighborhood's dismal heart, and walked through a blanket of humid air, passing the boarded-up Kingstanding Pub, which was covered in graffiti. I searched my memory bank and couldn't recall seeing a boarded-up pub in my extensive travels in the British Isles. I walked by a semi-deserted shopping center, a realty office advertising homes in the £120,000–£180,000 range, and a cavernous bingo and slot machine parlor called Mecca King, where I met Ziggy, an Indian bus driver who was taking a smoke break beside his bus. I asked him to tell me about the neighborhood and he cringed, a pained expression drifting across his cherubic face.

"This area's not too good," he said. "I live up in Sutton Coldfield. Much better."

I was under the impression we were in Sutton Coldfield but he corrected me. "Kingstanding," he said, glancing around to see if anyone was listening to us in the roundabout. "Very different."

Ziggy said I had to meet Ken, a regular at a betting parlor called Betfred across the traffic circle. "He knows everything 'bout this area," he promised.

I followed him into Betfred and a black man named Lee with cornrows said, "Ken usually doesn't come in till round eleven." Ziggy got back on his bus and I repaired to a busy little place called Benny's Diner, where I ordered the most expensive item on the menu—the full super English breakfast, a bargain at £4.50. I sat outside in the shade, listening to a pair of generously proportioned women of middle age complain about the men in their lives. "Eees in ab-suh-loot fookin nob," said the larger one, apparently remarking on her friend's significant other, as I started in on my black pudding, nearly always the salty highlight of any English breakfast.

I walked a few blocks in the surprisingly menacing heat, passing the massive bingo parlor, to see William's childhood home, which was located directly behind the parking lot. It was a modest, red-brick affair, attached to another dwelling, with a pair of potted plants at the doorway and a parched lawn that was full of dandelions. The windows were mostly open, the trash was at the curb, and there was a blue Mitsubishi Colt parked in the driveway. Tim Wood told me that the family didn't want to speak to me. Badgering uncooperative sources at their homes isn't my style so I didn't knock.

William's childhood home ©Dave Seminara

While in England, Wood and I spoke on the phone and exchanged many texts. On July 16, he wrote:

> William doesn't live here, and his family, here and elsewhere, really really want nothing to do with any of this stuff. However we can meet for a quick drink at a pub in Sutton… if you want. My condition would be that we meet for no more than an hour at a pub of my choosing and that you agree not to bother his family at all…Also, I today received a letter from William with instructions to pass it on to you. It's his first and only statement on all that has happened.

I wasn't planning to "bother" his family anyways, so this wasn't an issue for me, even though I do not, as a practice, negotiate interviews in this fashion. Wood never met with me, and when I asked him to email or text me the letter, so I could see it before visiting his neighborhood, he said he would. But then later when I asked him to follow through, he wrote, "William specifically instructed that it [the letter] be posted or given in person." Since I was in England and wouldn't be home for weeks, I had no idea if a letter existed or what it might entail.

There's a visceral difference between reading about a supposedly working-class area and actually walking the streets there, seeing the decrepitude and despair, experiencing, even if briefly, how life is lived.

After spending a morning in Kingstanding, it was easy to understand why William was dreaming about the Kapingamarangis of the world. He lived close enough to a posh area to see that there was a brighter side to life. Seeing his neighborhood provided some essential context to what had driven him and what had perhaps inspired his wanderlust.

After my late breakfast at Benny's I ducked into a stifling hot YMCA charity shop near the roundabout, where the lone customer in the place, a young woman with red hair and an oversized hat, was buying an "I Love [heart symbol] London" t-shirt for thirty pence. (Birmingham is England's second-largest city, so this was a bit like encountering someone in LA buying an "I Love NY" t-shirt, but I suspected it was the price that enticed her.) I struck up a conversation with a sweaty, portly young man named Connor wearing Coke-bottle glasses, too-tight black jeans, and a black *Call of Duty* t-shirt. I asked him what there was to do in the area.

"Not much," he said.

"Well, what do you do?" I asked.

"Well," he said, "I volunteer ear. I'm into gaming, noot mooch else. There's a library I go to."

He offered to show me the library—"Nothin' better to do, I suppose," he explained—and we walked off into the sun-drenched streets together.

"Why uh yuh ear?" he asked.

I explained my mission and he, like several others I'd asked, said he'd never heard of William. "Duh yuh luh-ike England?" he asked.

"Love it," I said.

He found this bizarre. "I 'ate it ear," he said.

He complained that the weather was always too hot or too cold and said that there was nothing to do.

"Eyed loik to go soomwhere else," he said. "Where?" I asked.

"Anywhere."

I asked Connor what Kingstanding was known for.

"It's not really known for anneh thing," he said after a few moments' reflection. "It's just kinda ear."

CHAPTER 17
◇◇◇◇◇◇◇◇◇

Pen Pals

I always feel that I am a traveler, going some-
where and to some destination. If I tell myself that
the somewhere and the destination do not exist, that
seems to me very likely and reasonable enough.

—VINCENT VAN GOGH

I arrived back in Oregon a few weeks after my UK trip and was surprised to find a large envelope from Tim Wood containing a small, thick, high-quality stationery envelope with typewritten print that read, "F.A.O. DAVE SEMINARA." I haven't received a letter prepared on a typewriter in at least twenty-five years, so I was immediately intrigued. It was a typewritten letter from William:

Dear Dave,

I feel that now may be an appropriate time to break the silence I have maintained since last

November. Enough speculation and myth has
[sic] been taken for truth already, so I wish to
lay out a few truths myself, directly.

William directed me to Wood's earlier, vague explanation on
the name change, which was that it had to do with a family matter. He maintained that it was "never my intention to defraud anyone," and concluded that it was his poor management that led to
his business floundering. William claimed that he was repaying his
creditors and organizing new (promised) trips, including one to the
remote (mostly off-limits) Brazilian islands of Trindade and Martin
Vaz in January 2019. (Note: these did not take place.)

"Is this a new beginning for me in business?" he asked.
"Potentially—although I would not say that it is a priority at
the moment."

Baekeland vaguely alluded to a "number of other business ventures" he was involved in but said that having to defend himself against criminal allegations in multiple jurisdictions was draining his time and resources.

On the question of wanderlust, William claimed that he had a very "international" upbringing and had lived in a few countries. He railed against the "gutter-press," which he said had mischaracterized his background, and referred to some of his early trips around Europe, which peaked his interest in travel.

> "The reality is rather simple, there is nothing which I find to be too boring to see or do or learn. This lifelong mentality has been of great benefit to me. It may well explain why I have been very content to travel of my own volition to countries such as Somalia and South Sudan multiple times each."

William wrote that around the age of fourteen or fifteen he became interested in seeing the "last vestiges" of the British Empire and visiting "all of the countries and colonies of the world."

He outlined his list of twelve thousand places he wants to visit and represented himself as a young man with the means to travel, but didn't explain where the money came from. William said that once he resolved his legal problems he would resume with his "more difficult travel goals."

Baekeland said that he hasn't lived in the UK since 2011 and claimed that he would be "sailing" to New York City later in 2018 for "business and other matters." He concluded, "People who know me closely would perhaps describe me as someone with a highly developed sense of privacy and a lack of interest in the thoughts and intrusions of the outside world." The salutation read, "May the emblem of Light illuminate you, William S. Baekeland," and the signature read, "William" with no surname, as though he was LeBron or Pelé or Bono.

I felt like the letter was written by a young man who was still in character, playing the part of the rich young aristocrat. I wrote back asking him to step out of character and tell me what role wanderlust had played in landing him in his present situation.

While I waited for this unlikely explanation, I finished Mitsidis's book, which concludes with an anecdote, told by "John," a young man who Mitsidis says once had a fling with William. John claimed that, as a teen, William used to dress up in a suit and buy a first-class train ticket and ride back and forth, over and over again, from Birmingham to Coventry (a twenty-minute ride), in order to study how wealthy travelers acted and, perhaps, live out his fantasy.

"He was thinking and observing and planning so that when the time finally came, when he would meet people who didn't have any reference point to who he really is, he would be convincing," Mitsidis wrote. "He would be the elegant man from those fabulous posh estates where he always believed he belonged. He would finally be the real thing."

❖   ❖   ❖

A few months after visiting his hometown, a friend sent me an email with an update on the Irish police's investigation of William's schemes. According to the source, the police were still investigating William, who had secured an attorney. He had reportedly changed his name again and had moved back to another residence at the K Club in Ireland. The police source believed that William had moved on to a new occupation: selling South African diamonds to the Asian market.

I wondered how my extreme travel friends would get to some of their bucket list destinations with William out of the game. One day in October 2018, I went to the MTP website and saw an intriguing notice on the homepage: an advertisement for a new expedition to Bouvet, run by a group of ham radio enthusiasts. (Another similar group was forced to abort their mission after spending three days in January 2018 battling hurricane-force winds off of Bouvet that prevented them from landing.)

I reckoned that hope was eternal, with or without Mr. Baekeland. But the expedition failed. The travelers sighted Bouvet, just as William and the gang had, but sixty-to-seventy-knot winds and "angry seas" kept them at bay. Alas, they are fundraising to try again in December 2020.

Despite many assurances from William's consigliere that he planned to respond to my questions, I reckoned that I'd never hear from him again as the weeks dragged into months. But right before Christmas, I got a large airmail envelope from an address (with no name) just outside Birmingham. I tore it open like a child hoping for a golden ticket to Willy Wonka's Chocolate Factory, assuming that I was soon to be on the receiving end of a dose of travel wisdom from the Dalai Lama of Extreme Travel, Sir William Baekeland, or whatever the hell his name is. But alas, it was a Christmas card with a beautifully sketched drawing of Christmas Island on the cover.

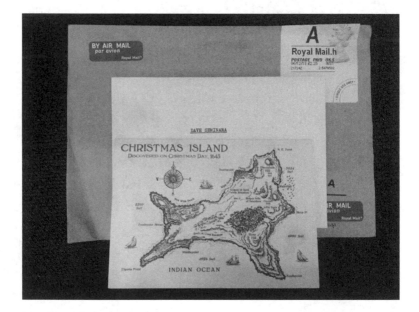

Christmas Island of Australia, not Christmas Island of Kiribati..!

December 2018.

Dave,

Wishing you and your family a very happy Christmas and a pleasant year ahead. I wish you successful travels and writing...

with warm wishes,
William

Dave,

Wishing you and your family a very happy
Christmas and a pleasant year ahead. I wish you
successful travels and writing…

With warm wishes,
William

On the flip page inside the map of Christmas Island, there was a note betraying the fact that William remained a traveler to the end: "Christmas Island of Australia, not Christmas Island of Kiribati!"

Once more, I assumed that I'd never hear from William again but in early February, I got a text from his consigliere. "A present should have landed in your inbox. Apologies for the delay." I checked my email and found a four-page letter, dated February 5, 2019 with a dateline of Simla, India. Simla, also spelled Shimla, is known for its British-built Kalka-Shimla railway line, an UNESCO World Heritage site, and its wealth of British Colonial architecture, so it didn't surprise me that William would be interested in spending time there.

William cryptically claimed that he had previously sent me a package I hadn't received with "things in it that may have been of interest" without specifying what those things were. The letter contained twelve numbered points, mostly critiques of Harry Mitsidis and his "opus, which in his mind surely has the likes of Agatha Christie and Arthur Conan Doyle smoking nervously on the sideline," William wrote. "Hercule Poirot, he most certainly is not."

William's most strenuous objections to Harry's book revolved around the homosexual affair allegations, particularly in the last chapter, where Harry alleges that William had relations with "John" a childhood friend, when he was a minor. "He has accused me of being a child sex offender," William wrote. "John is the biggest mythomaniac you could hope to meet. He is a self- aggrandizing liar."

In William's final numbered point (number twelve), he concludes, "Harry has overegged his pudding now." He asserted that he's taking legal action against Harry for the book and segued into a section where he took a few parting shots at the country collectors who helped finance his travel ambitions in recent years. About one notable traveler he wrote, "He's a bored millionaire who decided to attach his pseudo- alpha male competitiveness, his "locker room mindset" to the field of extreme travel.... He knows the price of everything and the value of nothing."

Speaking more broadly about the country-collecting group, he wrote, "Most are relatively superficial and uninteresting people.... For the most part, being involved with such a neurotic group has been a burden, not a benefit or a joy." He concluded the letter by summarizing his plans:

> Later in the year I'll be back in Europe, and, after wedding my bride in London, I will spend most of my time in Italy. Following this, I have a few fixed plans in Africa, the United States, and of course, India. I have an expedition organized and fixed for the end of the year in Antarctica to the peninsula and Peter I Island—an island [on which] I failed to land on my birthday in 2017. This time, however, I am not making the mistake of taking other "travellers" along with me. Finally, I trust you have been reading the British "press" and have your intellect to figure out how I fit into one of its foremost stories.
>
> May you find what you seek, WILLIAM

I assumed he was referring to Brexit but could only guess if he planned to stay in India after his peregrinations. India has an extradition treaty with the UK, but not with Ireland, where police were reportedly investigating his dealings with extreme travelers. William failed to respond to the question I most wanted him to address: How had his wanderlust gotten him into the mess he was in? I wrote back and a couple weeks later Tim emailed me another letter from William, composed on a typewriter and dated February 9, 2019, with the dateline Simla, India:

> Later on in the year I will indeed be married, to a woman. This is far from a surprise to those who actually know me. As for what others think, I am not in the slightest bit interested. I'm not going to bother criticising Harry [Mitsidis] further about this, and I am not insisting either way what Harry has or hasn't said about me, as it doesn't bother me. His own insecurities bother him far more and he clearly revels in projecting these onto others. It is a typical trait of him in general, from my observation and experience.

> Furthermore, if Harry is so insistent that I am [a] sociopathic liar, why does he still pick and choose what he believes about me or what I may or may not have said to him over a period of time? It is irrational, and I laugh at the absurdity of it all.

After the wedding we will travel to Switzerland and Austria for a few weeks before ending up in Italy, to be a new home. My grandmother is Italian, and I also lived there several hundred years ago, in an age when pepper had value. My travel plans and the "situation" with the creditors are not linked. I have already repaid some of my creditors, this is a matter of fact. Whether or not they have chosen to broadcast this to the world a la Harry or not is not something I can confirm, as I don't know or care.

I made considerable repayments to various creditors BEFORE Harry's "Apocalypse" eMail, as well as after. Nevertheless, I remain committed to making full financial resolutions when the legal situation created by a select few concludes. To do so beforehand would be improper and against my legal advice.

Furthermore, a number of creditors have made false claims of debt owed by myself, some have made reports of those false claims to the police and I am completely disinclined to engage with those people. A number of people actually owe me considerable sums of money as per contractual agreements which are recorded and binding. I am undecided as to whether I will bother pursing those debts through the civil courts or not.

Regarding the travel plans referenced, they are not inexpensive, but they are time efficient as per my systematic travel concept and the self imposed time restrictions placed on them. Nothing in Antarctica is especially cheap or certain, as I said, I already failed to land on Peter I Island in 2017, but I was on a scheduled cruise and they had very strict schedules to keep to– there was no flexibility factored into their programme. With Antarctica it is vital to factor in for bad weather and the unknown in general.

There is no way I could ever consider inviting other travellers to join any such expedition again, to share or reduce costs, or to profit. Until 2017 I was more than happy to do so as the planets Mercury and Saturn were not in an adverse conjunction with any other body. As this is no longer so, it is unthinkable, and I am rather glad for it.

It was a successful system until 2017, and as predicted by a numerologist I corresponded with nine years prior, it did indeed come to a sudden end after a single cycle of seven years. As you are no doubt aware, seven is the most sacred of numbers and has many special attributes, which I won't bother with her[e] as it's no doubt out with your interest for the purposes of your book. The significance of certain numbers, you will find from your own study though, probably has a serious influence on the wanderlust of many people, including myself.

Feel free to ask to clarify [any of] that. Kind wishes to you from wintery Simla…

WILLIAM

It seemed like William was rather enjoying sparring with me and probably hoped that I'd get his side of the story out. But it was hard to follow his game plan. If he wanted to advance the narrative that he was trying to repay his creditors, why reference all of his elaborate and expensive travel plans? I asked more follow-up questions but heard nothing until I got an email from Tim in September 2019:

> Things are going fairly well, I must say, at least for the moment. William, meanwhile, is expanding the stone business in Africa; frankly, it is a much better suit for him than the travel business was. He is able to traverse the globe, dealing with precious stones and planning for his upcoming nuptuals [sic].
>
> It's all gone a little quiet on the creditor front, and I think the likely best course is for us and them to maintain this. So, as far as lawsuits go I've advised William (and decided myself as well) to keep a little powder dry: Harry

probably knew he was overstepping a few boundaries, hence his decision to pseudo-anonymise myself and even William in the book. Hopefully, a line can be drawn under everything soon.

Compensation has been paid to three travellers, yes. Not the full sums due but considerable amounts nonetheless, and William is aiming to pay further compensation on an ad hoc basis. Harry, of course, volunteered to go last in receiving a penny and I'm sure William intends to take him up on his beneficent offer to his fellow creditors.

So it seemed as though the lawsuits William had threatened never materialized. I knew of only one traveler—Babis Bizas—who was refunded so I asked Tim to let me know who else was repaid but he never responded. Was William really slinging stones? And who was the mystery bride? We may never know. But though I never got an answer to the question about repayments, William did respond very promptly via Tim to a question I sent regarding Bruce Chatwin. I asked him whether he liked Chatwin's work because I (correctly) assumed that he'd be familiar with Chatwin's theory that people should be nomadic.

In the typewritten letter, dated October 12, 2019, and now with the dateline "BOULOGNE-SUR-MER, FRANCE" in all caps, Baekeland said that he found my query interesting and wrote that he wasn't a fan of Chatwin:

His theories of the best way humans live is somewhat unusual but relatable to an extent—I have the desire to roam very much as you know...He took the view that man is meant to be nomadic and that this is the natural state. I am very much a home lover also and I feel this being something which is stronger in me now—to a certain extent anyway. I firmly believe that people need a stable rooted existence outside of travel...Man is destined to build and have purpose, and to forever roam is the antithesis of this—it is the ultimate in self-serving vanity only.

I look at almost all of the other travelers that I used to know and see this in them and I did from the very onset of my involvement with all of them.

It's interesting to say the least that a young man who had not so long ago sent these people a Christmas card detailing his dizzying travel schedule along with statistics on the number of flights he took and so on was now aiming this sort of a loaded weapon in their direction. And when he says he saw this character flaw in them, can we assume that this perceived vulnerability made them appealing targets?

Leading a life like them is something I never wanted and certainly don't now. How many of them are married, stable, happy with their fam-

ilies, happy with life at home, integrated into
[a] sort of meaningful and tangible community
(their self claimed community of travelers is
really anything but)[?] …Perhaps they cannot
see it so well from their insular perspective…
Most of them are faithless wanderers with very
little else in their lives.

He went on to call the travels of Chatwin and the extreme travelers "baseless pilgrimages without any end point":

The metaphysical aspect of travel for Chatwin
(as well as the travelers) ultimately has no purpose other than the gratification of the self,
[and] it is therefore meaningless…To me this
is a completely wasted way to live life…I can
only hope that my travels through God's glori-
ous Eden bring for me a greater metaphysical
purpose to my actions, and show others the
right way in the process.

If this epistle from St. William wasn't odd enough, he closed
the letter by expressing his admiration for the British writer Lisa St.
Aubin de Terán, whom he described as "zany and mercurial," and
signing off with a cryptic reference to her work.

Baekeland wrote that he admired her "fragmented and strange
background and the erratic patterns in the way she has chosen to
live her life." Perhaps he was referring to her 1998 memoir *The
Hacienda*, which describes how she fell into a whirlwind marriage
to a Venezuelan and lived for seven years on a remote farm in the
Andean region of Venezuela, or her 2007 memoir *Mozambique*

Mysteries, which covers a period when she moved to Africa to set up a charity? She also wrote a memoir detailing her life as a train addict, a collection called *The Virago Book of Wanderlust and Dreams*, which begins with a memorable passage: "Traveling is like flirting with life. It's like saying, 'I would stay and love you but I have to go, this is my station.'"

William signed off, writing, "The ultimate reason for my great interest in her literature is something which will perhaps not come to the light of the world until a couple of decades hence. I will be sure to write to you and let you know when that moment gloriously and blessedly comes."

I wrote to William's favorite author, via a charity she runs in Mozambique, to ask her for help in decoding the reference, but she didn't respond. I tried again seven months later, in May 2020, and quickly received a reply with the name Lisa de Terán Duff-Scott:

Dear Dave,

I am sitting at home in Mozambique (where I have lived for the past 15 years) wondering which of my 19 books he is referring to.

In some ways, the most contentious book I have written is 'Otto[,]' a semi-fictionalized biography of the late Osvaldo Barreto Miliani, the Venezuelan scholar, Professor of Sociology, Author and revolutionary (and my dearest friend). There is a lot of behind the scenes political content in the book taken from verbatim interviews with Osvaldo, code name 'Otto'. These include some major mid 20th Century figures.

Other than that, I can't imagine what he means unless it is in connection with my name, which is not my name at all really. I was born Lisa Carew, my mother changed my name by Deed Poll when I was 12 to St. Aubin (a name chosen for no better reason than that she was born in St. Aubin in Jersey), then I married Jaime Teran and added on the de Teran as Spanish law dictates, but then I left Jaime Teran but kept his name as Spanish law does not dictate. When I was married to the Scottish poet, George Macbeth, I was also Lisa Macbeth, and then I married the painter Robbie Duff-Scott and I am now officially still Lisa Duff-Scott e.g. on my passport although I left Robbie 19 years ago and he died at the end of 2017. Maybe a con man likes all the name changes. Other than that, I really can't help you.

Good luck with your book. And, as I live in the sticks, I would love you to email me a copy when you have finished it because I languish here for lack of books and being old school, I cannot bring myself to use a Kindle. In my old age, there is nothing I like more than a good new book.

Best wishes from Lisa etc.

This made my day. Of course William would love a writer who loved train travel and had changed names more times than he had. And the fact that even the author had no idea what he was talking about tickled me. (William later told me that Lisa etc.'s presumptions were incorrect but he declined to comment further.) But as peculiar as this letter was, nothing could have prepared me for the eighteen-page typewritten missive I received a couple weeks later. The letter was, on the one hand, filled with bible verses, but on the other the nastiest invective I have ever read, mostly directed at Harry Mitsidis, thanks to his book, Dominique Laurent, who was the only victim still pursuing William in the courts and via the media, and the broader community of extreme travelers. (Mr. Laurent helped orchestrate an article in the French newspaper *Le Parisien* that particularly galled William.)

Filled with the most vulgar, homophobic, anti-Semitic language imaginable, it was difficult to read. William used the word "whore" dozens of times throughout the letter and he repeatedly railed against "globalist feminist...faggots," "evil Talmudic plots," and the like. I'm only going to include a few quotes, without names attached, to represent the vile spirit of this letter:

> Her adultery will end up costing her life ultimately, and Mr. Laurent continues to help fund her sybaritic existence. She adorns herself caked in unsightly makeup, doing all within her powers to make herself look like more of a slut, to attract whoremongering heathens to her door...God's WILL is escaped by nobody, and her refusal to repent, and to go on with her adulterous and murdering ways will end

in total damnation for her sorry self. We will be praying for God to do justice upon this wretched whore...she is probably a Talmudic bitch of Moloch, his personal French whoring slut, going out unto the world to do his evil.

Globalist whoremonger doer of evil.

Portugal is a filthy unholy land full of twisted evil and sodomite sin. It is x's favorite country.

He is a greedy, idolatrous, sodomising, voracious beast.

We will also pray for ALL Lufthansa aircraft to crash into the new World Trade Centre in the American city of Sodom, New JEW York... Just as those towers came down in 2001 to punish America in the same way, along with Lufthansa, being an apparatus of Germany which is another abominable unholy land.

William interspersed bible verses and warnings that various people would burn in hell, often in caps, throughout the disgusting, unhinged letter and near the end, bizarrely claimed that he would be returning to Ireland with his family to start a church, of all things, so he could "pray in peace" for the extreme travelers. "You are very much welcome and invited to join us in worship and praise of God if you find yourself in Ireland in the future," he wrote.

I shared a few pages of the letter with Dominique, who had just returned from climbing the highest mountain in India and had a bad cough. "Maybe he is really creating a church, it's a scam to get more money," he said, before altering course. "No, no, he's trying to be crazy. He disguises himself as a lunatic to create his insanity defense, this must be it."

The Frenchman said the way the accusations against William snowballed, with more and more victims coming forward as time went on, was like the Me Too movement. "Not that I'm comparing what we went through to them," he said. The Frenchman said he didn't expect to get a penny from the proceedings but still wanted justice to be done. "I want him to be punished," he said. "He deserves that."

On the one hand, I found William's disturbing letter painful to read. But on the other, I felt like perhaps it offered a ray of hope for William's creditors. If he was preparing an insanity defense, he must have felt that the wheels of justice were coming his way.

CHAPTER 18

◇◇◇◇◇◇◇◇◇

Curse of the Nomads

A change in the weather is sufficient to recreate the world and ourselves.

—MARCEL PROUST

In his entertaining book, *The Geography of Madness: Penis Thieves, Voodoo Death, and the Search for the Meaning of the World's Strangest Syndromes*, the travel writer Frank Bures relates a telling anecdote from the English philosopher Herbert Spencer, who wrote of a Frenchman who wanted to write a book about England after being there for three weeks. As the story goes, after three months the hapless Frenchman wasn't quite ready to put pen to paper. After living there for three years, he gave up, concluding that he knew nothing about England at all. *Sacrébleu!*

When I first met Don Parrish in 2014, he had just thirty-six places left to visit on the MTP list, having hit 838 targets on what was then an 874-place list. By the end of 2018, he had just twenty-two spots left to visit in order to finally complete the list. Mind you, whittling this list down is hard work as it contains off-limits places and superbly hard-to-reach destinations like the Chesterfield Islands, in the middle of the Pacific, Marie Byrd Land, in the Antarctic, and so on.

I corresponded with Don in February 2019 while he was in Mexico, where he planned to visit twenty UNESCO World Heritage sites in two weeks. He had some annoying news to share: Charles Veley had expanded the MTP list to include nineteen new places as a "Christmas gift." He had already visited just four of the new sites. And so, after five years of arduous travel, his MTP target list had grown from thirty-six places to thirty-seven. The good news, he said, was that two once forbidden islands—Nicobar (Bay of Bengal) and Paracel (South China Sea)—were opening up. And so, there was always somewhere to go.

The quest to understand the world is a noble one, but it's also futile. This doesn't mean that we should be content to stay put. Hell no! I derive energy and inspiration from movement and change. But William's story was a cautionary tale for me. I could see how wanderlust and the thirst for adventure infected both William and his victims. For some, the pursuit of everywhere is noble; for others, it is self-serving vanity.

That said, delving deep into the world of country collecting has also confirmed my conviction that I'm simply not cut out to stay home. I'm too curious, too hyperactive, too much of a novelty seeker to stay put for very long. I can learn something from content homebodies, but I cannot and *will not* become one of them. My tribe is my tribe.

Is this because I have the 7R allele, the so-called nomadic gene, rendering me genetically predisposed to wandering and novelty seeking? As it turns out, no. When I received the news via my DRD4 test from the Mayo Clinic that I have two copies of the (more common) 4R allele, and zero copies of the 7R allele, I was disappointed. I immediately thought back to studies I'd read about 4Rs, describing them as cautious, rigid, and low on the novelty-seeking spectrum. I'm nothing like that so I assumed that there was no way I could be a 4R. But now I had the results on paper that I was "4/4" from the world's leading medical facility and they made no sense to me.

My dopamine receptor DRD4 genotyping test

My wife thought the test result was good news, but I didn't want to hear it. I wanted to understand wanderlust and, based on everything I'd read, I felt like heredity was an important component of it. I was sure I was a 7R. I wanted to be a 7R, probably because it's easier to blame some of the dodgier decisions I've made on genetics—it's in my blood!—rather than my own life choices.

I contacted Luke Matthews, the professor who had described describe high-novelty-seeking 4Rs as "rigid, prudent, stoic, reflective, staid, and slow-tempered," in a paper I had read. I told him that I'm none of these things.

"There are multiple genes that affect these personality traits, and the genes interact with each other and with life experiences," he wrote back. "At an aggregate population level, like in my 2011 paper, you can find an overall average correlation between genes and their associated personality traits, but for any specific individual any particular gene might not be strongly correlated with their personality."

Indeed, heritability is a complex picture and the fact that I'm a 4R doesn't mean that I haven't inherited any genes that might help explain my restlessness. But I still felt like my quest for answers had hit a roadblock until I emailed my friend, Megan Fernandez, who has followed my journey.

"You don't need it [7R] to validate your status as a traveler," she wrote. "The truth is in your experience, not in a test result, so it brings you back to the source of truth. Experience is the only truth. You were going to derive meaning from one test result, but you have a lifetime of meaning to use instead."

It only took me a heartbeat to realize that she was right. The Mayo Clinic had done me a favor. If the test had shown that I had one or even two copies of the 7R allele, my quest would have felt like an open-and-shut case that had reached its conclusion. Wandering is in our blood or it isn't. The fact that I'm a 4R—part of the majority—told me that the truth is more complex.

THE FOUL-TASTING FOUNTAIN OF YOUTH

On Easter Sunday, March 27, 1513, Juan Ponce de León sighted what he thought was an island at 30°8' that he named "La Florida" or "Place of Flowers," because it was close to the "festival of flowers," or Pascua Florida, and perhaps as a reference to the new flowering he hoped to experience from the fabled Fountain of Youth. Ponce, who is thought to have accompanied Christopher Columbus on his second voyage to the New World in 1493, was then the governor of Puerto Rico, and had orders from Spain's King Ferdinand to colonize a legendary, paradisal island called Bimini, supposedly home to the Fountain of Youth.

Most historians dispute this, but a smattering of more fun-loving ones think that Ferdinand, who had recently married a woman thirty-five years his junior, told Ponce to be on the lookout for the supposedly transformative fountain. At the time, such a mandate wouldn't have been viewed as completely ludicrous. Alexander the Great, for example, was said to have discovered a healing "river of paradise" in the fourth century B.C and similar legends have cropped up all over the world since.

For example, during the Middle Ages, some Europeans believed in the mythical King Prester John, a legendary Christian patriarch and king who was said to rule over a lost Christian nation—perhaps in India, Central Asia, or Ethiopia—whose kingdom supposedly boasted a fountain of youth and a river of gold, among other cool stuff.

Ponce never wrote about discovering a fountain of youth, as far as we know, and his final colonization attempt in La Florida, in 1821, didn't end well—he was mortally wounded when natives shot him in the thigh with an arrow poisoned with the sap of a manchineel tree. But after his death, a number of authors, including a few of his rivals, helped build the legend that old Ponce was looking for the fountain. In 1535 Gonzalo Fernández de Oviedo y Valdés accused Ponce de León of seeking the fountain in order to cure his sexual impotence. (Ponce fathered several children so this is highly unlikely.)

The legend is still alive, despite the historical uncertainty. And St. Augustine locals have been promoting a spring near where Ponce landed as the legendary Fountain of Youth since at least the nineteenth century. In 1909, Luella Day "Diamond Lil" McConnell, a Chicago physician who made a fortune during the Klondike Gold Rush, began to market "Fountain of Youth" water that some maintain was from a well dug in 1875, and charge admission to her Fountain of Youth site near where Ponce first landed.

I turned up at the Ponce de León Fountain of Youth Archaeological Park on the second day of 2019. I was on a new home base scouting trip with my wife, Jen, my sons, Leo and James, and my parents. St. Augustine was the third of four stops and I broke away from the group late in the afternoon when everyone else's energy level was spent to visit the fountain.

The street adjacent to the park has a canopy of majestic magnolia trees, which provide a suitable air of drama for those, like me, who want to believe they're entering a transformative place. The lush fifteen-acre grounds overlook the Matanzas River and St. Augustine Inlet and preening peacocks strut around the grounds along with silly-looking reenactors in period costumes. I imagined that the fountain would be outside, but, alas, it's in a brightly lit, sad room and has a stone sign hanging overhead: "THE FOUNTAIN OF YOUTH—This spring was discovered in 1513 and was recorded a landmark in a Spanish grant."

Three trickling streams of water flowed from underneath a large stone hearth and there were towers of plastic cups nearby for those who wanted to have a drink. I watched a group of laughing Russian-speaking tourists take photos of each other while gulping the waters. In the corner of the room, a woman of late middle age in tight khaki pants delivered a speech about Ponce and the fountain in a dreadful monotone voice as I waited my turn to get a taste.

> "He was here to find a new island, explore it,
> and colonize it. He claimed this area for Spain
> in 1513. He was here for five days and then he
> moved on."

As she droned on, I thought about what had brought me to this kitschy place. I was in Saint Augustine for one day less than Ponce, which isn't a lot of time to evaluate whether you want to live in a place. We were roughly midway through our trip. I had enjoyed every bit of it. But I always enjoy trips. How would I feel about living in Florida? At forty-six was I chasing my own fountain of youth by dragging my family across the country in a quite possibly futile bid to escape the health problems I'd suffered in Oregon? Ponce's quest felt unsettlingly familiar.

I drank the water and stood around for a few moments waiting to feel younger. It had a strong, acrid taste and I couldn't help wonder if the foul water was a metaphor for my quest.

In July 2019, we sold our house in Oregon, put most of our possessions in storage, and moved to St. Petersburg, Florida. The plan was to buy a house, yet we spent a month searching for the right place and didn't find one. Frustrated, I did what I always do in moments of crisis—I booked a trip, in this case a fifteen-day jaunt to Colombia. The trip was a revelation; every day was a reminder of why I crave and relish foreign travel.

But when we got back to Florida, the house hunt didn't get any easier. Everything in our price range was either in a sketchy neighborhood or was the neglected home of some geezer who just croaked. We spent six months living out of our suitcases in a small apartment overlooking Boca Ciega Bay. I was perfectly content, as it felt almost like a trip. But the kids started school and didn't have most of their toys and other stuff. It was a stressful situation for them. One day, my twelve-year-old son Leo said, "You don't like any houses, you always find something wrong with them. We're going to be stuck here in this little apartment forever."

The truth is that I love to live out of a suitcase and I didn't miss my belongings. Perhaps I was being too picky because I wanted to be living life like the country collectors. But eventually we bought a house—an older one that needed a lot of work. I adore the place but does that mean I want to stay there fifty-two weeks per year? Hell no!

I know that fleeing to Florida won't cure my health problems. And I don't want to be like Colonel Burton, hustling my family from one place to the next like a band of gypsies searching for a fountain of youth. In his book on Nile River explorers, Tim Jeal reports that Burton "regretted that his peripatetic life left him rootless and unattached." I don't want my children to feel the same way.

Before we had embarked on the scouting trips to Florida, my ten-year-old, James, said something that made me want to laugh and cry.

"I can't wait to get the hell out of here for good," I said, as we waddled penguin-like across our icy driveway to a taxi that would bring us to the airport.

"Dad, you always want to get the hell out of everywhere we go!" James said.

My ten-year-old son had just summarized my forty-six years on the planet in one prescient sentence and I had no idea how to respond. "It's true!" he continued, his voice rising. "We like Bend! I have all my friends here and my school!"

I wanted to reassure my son—tell him his impression of me was wrong. *I can change! I swear I can.* But instead I just gave him a hug and told him everything would be fine. I felt exposed, but there was no point in promising him that I would change my ways. I aspire to be more rooted, but at heart I'm a drifter and there's no use in pretending otherwise.

Burton understood the futility of his manic wandering but he also surrendered to the idea that it was in his nature. He said, "Man wants to wander and he must do so or he shall die," and that's the story of my life.

❖ ❖ ❖

While researching the Fountain of Youth, I stumbled across what seemed like an apt quote from Marcel Proust, from his seven-volume behemoth *In Search of Lost Time*, which has more than two thousand characters:

> The only true voyage of discovery, the only
> Fountain of Eternal Youth, would be not to
> visit strange lands but to possess other eyes,
> to behold the universe through the eyes of
> another, of a hundred others, to behold the
> hundred universes that each of them beholds,
> that each of them is.

Proust was a sick man. He started writing the book in 1909, at thirty-eight, and spent the last three years of his life largely confined to his room while completing the novel before he died at fifty-one of bronchitis and pneumonia. And so, visiting strange lands may have been impossible for him. I still have the ability to visit strange places, so the challenge to "possess other eyes" is an intriguing but unlikely prospect for me. In short, I'm not a Marcel Proust guy. I'm a "Let's go to strange lands" guy and I'm not going to change.

I started traveling as a young man and got hooked. There is a beauty and simplicity to the traveling lifestyle that makes it easy to be seduced. My obsession seems to always put me in the past, recalling past trips, and the future, where I'm going next, but often not in the present.

Why are some content to stay at home while others need to explore? For the same reason some of us like clam chowder and others don't. We're all hard wired differently. Some of us find stimulation at home or are better at suppressing the urge to travel.

Wanderlust is that dangerous itch that triggers the need for escape the way a starting pistol signals the beginning of a race. A light bulb goes on in your head and BANG! You've got to go.

My affinity for travel is much deeper and more complex than a simple need to escape. Good, bad, or somewhere in between, trips are always memorable. Days, weeks, months, and years can blend together when I'm at home. But I can remember days of travel very vividly years after the fact, and the experience of reliving these times invigorates me and inspires me to get back on the road.

The extreme travelers on the losing end of William's grandiose plans were vulnerable because they *really* wanted to get to forbidden places at the end of the world and William was their ticket, or at least he seemed to be. They'll be more cautious moving forward and some are introspective enough to understand that their wanderlust blinded them to the reality that Baekeland was too good to be true. But none of us are staying home because travel is what we do and it's part of who we are. Leo Tolstoy once expressed a sentiment that could apply to all of us, but particularly William, when he said, "Everyone thinks of changing the world, but no one thinks of changing himself."

EPILOGUE

◇◇◇◇◇◇◇

The best trips, like the best love affairs,
never really end.

—Pico Iyer

I was certain that the Baekeland affair, or at least my involvement in it, was over at the close of the last decade. But three weeks into 2020, I received a surprising email from someone named Jasmine, who claimed to be William's cousin:

> Hi Dave,
>
> William has asked me to answer any questions that you might have in relation to him and your book. I'm also in touch with the TV company in New York which is making a documentary about him and his work as you may know. He sends his best from Central Africa.
>
> Jasmine

I had ignored William's eighteen-page fire-and-brimstone letter and perhaps he was disappointed, bargaining that it was bound to provoke a response. The "tv company" she referred to is a production company called Jigsaw Productions that was producing a show about the Baekeland affair for HBO.

I had heard about the show through the extreme traveler grapevine, but it was news to me that William was planning to cooperate with them. A few travelers had told me that the film about William would be one episode in a series about con artists. I wrote back to Jasmine (or was it William?) to ask if the rambling, anti-Semitic letter was meant to pave the way for an insanity plea. She replied:

> The only thing I would point out is that he isn't going to be setting up an insanity defence. Rightly or wrongly he is of the view, and always was, that he has committed no crime and thus doesn't need a legal defence. All countries where a crime was reported have since confirmed to William's lawyers that they consider no crime committed and therefore no investigation ever happened. As you probably know Ireland was the only exception here and they since dropped that as a case. [Note: Dominique Laurent and others dispute this contention strenuously.]
>
> As for anti-[S]emitism, it just hasn't escaped his notice, and Tim has commented on it a few times as well, that four of the major ringleaders in this are Jews; [here she names an official William dealt with at the Nature

Conservancy), her nephew Sam Blum, who authored the first (*Rolling Stone*) article breaking the "story," Harry Mitsidis (who is Jewish via his mother), and one of the producers at HBO]... I haven't seen what he sent you, but I can still say that it can't be any more offensive or untrue than things said about William or our family in much more public settings. Regarding his participation in the HBO documentary, Jasmine wrote:

> The producers told William that they are not framing him as a conman... If the producers or others told you that the brief was about conmen then this is not true, either, and perhaps a plot to encourage cooperation of a few specific people. As I understand it, they are chiefly interested in filming William in situ at his various business and missionary projects in Africa.

Business and missionary projects indeed! I sent Jasmine a follow-up message and she clarified her understanding of what the show was to be about, sending me the text of what William allegedly received about the show from his contact at Jigsaw:

> HBO will showcase 10 stories of a new generation of "enterprising" young individuals from around the globe (so-called "millennials") as they chase their dreams in brilliant, creative and sometimes unconventional ways. For

reference, some other features include an Ivy League graduate who became a trusted financial advisor to elite athletes; a young woman who wrote a bestselling book and inspired an international wellness movement; a young man who began building a nightlife empire as a teenager; and a classical composer who improbably inspired a nation.

William Baekeland was going to be featured on HBO alongside a young composer who "improbably inspired a nation" and a young woman who "inspired an international wellness movement? It seemed wildly improbable but William was a charmer. Had he seduced these filmmakers as well?

One traveler remarked of the Jigsaw correspondence, "William Gordon—This is a nice choice of a name. I [have previously] dealt with Jesse Butcher, Simon Baekeland, and William Baekeland.... Possibly he will be able to sue HBO for some breach of contract and then have enough capital to beat off the travelers he conned."

I was excited that HBO was interested in the story because it validated my own fascination with it. I reached out to Jigsaw and eventually had a few conversations with their team. I came away from these meetings convinced that Jigsaw is endeavoring to provide a fair and accurate telling of this story, just as I am. William reportedly asked the filmmakers for a $2 million fee to appear on camera. They declined to pay him and so he's not in their film, which is called "Baekeland."

For her part, Jasmine said that I could ask William anything I wanted in a telephone interview. But then William followed up on February 24 with an email from an email address he'd never messaged me from before with the name William Gordon detailing his terms. "I will grant the interview on the sole condition that you elect to reference me in your chapter list and title by my current legal name (William Gordon) and make whatever commentary on previous changes within the content of the chapter text," he wrote.

I purposely changed his given family name in this book to protect his family's privacy and to forestall any pointless legal challenges from William. But I wasn't going to take the Baekeland name out of the book because it's integral to the story and I told him so. We corresponded back and forth over the next few days. What follows are some of the lowlights.

Key points of an email from William on February 25:

1. I am, and always have been, a collateral descendant of the Baekeland family in Belgium, who then went to America. This is a matter of public record. I will be taking further legal action against any other person who publishes claims to the contrary.

2. At no point whatsoever, during the course of any of my dealings with the travellers involved in the story which so captivates you, did I discuss money, my means, their means or any satellite matter to that subject. At no point can anyone recall an instance of it happening - because it did not. Only once was I ever asked directly about money, that was in private, by Don Parish, in May 2015, where he asked me directly if I was a billionaire. Surprised by this impertinence, I simply responded, truthfully, with "no". Any claims to the contrary were as a result of rumours started by the now dead serial gossip, Helmut Lent.

3. I am now in the early stages of several very large lawsuits against a number of people/organisations connected with this "case", so have no time whatsoever, for any further twisting of reality, misinformation or libels made against me. You may wonder why I have waited until now to commence this, and the answer is rather simple. Unlike a number of my adversaries, I do not allow heated passion to cloud judgement and [force] me to play my entire hand in one immediate, poorly executed go.

4. Whilst I will not insist on it, I strongly urge you to send a copy of your relevant chapters about me to my lawyers for them to review for any accidental libels made against me. I will gladly offer you that at my expense - their time is not cheap.

5. Recently I have spent several days showing the HBO film team around my home in England, Scotland and various sites relating to my childhood and family members. If you would like me to ensure that your book is mentioned in the documentary, please let me know the final details of it and when it will be available, if you know yet. The expected audience size is 20m+. Whilst I do not wish to, nor will, profit financially from this ridiculous saga, I do not care if others wish to - as long as that is not at the expense of accuracy, truth and quality.

As soon as I read his contention that he's a member of the Baekeland family, I knew that William was unfortunately still in bullshit mode. I had, perhaps naively, hoped that he might be ready to tell me the truth, or at least his version of it. It was clear that the talk of lawyers (and plural "lawyers" at that!) and lawsuits was meant to intimidate me. The reference to HBO and its audience of twenty million—obviously made before he decided not to appear on camera in their film—was intended to entice me with a potential marketplace for this book. The broader point was clear: let me vet your book and I'll help you sell it.

Here are excerpts from my response:

> You say that it's a matter of public record that you're a Baekeland descendant. I'm happy to look at whatever evidence you have on this but I corresponded with a Baekeland family historian who produced a documentary on Leo Baekeland and he says that he seriously doubts this. Are you claiming that you're a direct descendant of Leo Baekeland? If so, please explain the connection.

> I have listened to the interview you gave to *Counting Countries*, I read the Christmas card you sent travelers a few years ago, I reviewed the interview you gave to Harry for his newsletter, and I've reviewed dozens and dozens of emails that you've sent to travelers. You never explicitly stated, "I am a billionaire," but you gave the impression that you came from a lot of money. And obviously few 20-somethings who don't have $$$$ are taking cruises to Bouvet Island and doing all the other trips you were doing.

You told [Ric] Gazarian that your family stayed at the Pink Palace in Hawaii every year and said that as a youth you traveled back and forth to Prague for (was it cello?) lessons. [Note: it was actually harp.] You boasted of your family's philanthropic connections, which paved the way for your visit to Palmyra. Your Christmas card is full of outlandish boasts and outright lies. In everything you said and did, you gave travelers the impression that you came from money and didn't have to work for a living. I've been to Kingstanding, William, so all of this is, as I think they say in your country, bollocks.

Finally, I'd like you to read what Tim, your con-sigliere, wrote after the scandal broke. If you've done absolutely nothing wrong, why would he have written these words: "So, you all know who I am, in time you will learn that I did not play a knowing part in William's trickery, and can decide whether you ever wish to transact with my company for trips in the future; I will of course understand if none of you do. William's future is uncertain at the moment, and, as we all know, he faces the prospect of a custodial sentence if convicted in relation [to] this missing money.

I will probably never really understand why he did this, why he took a skill and a viable business organising trips and ruined it for the sake of ego and greed....Once again, it is terribly sad that I find myself writing this email, and terribly sad that you find yourselves, through no fault of your own, reading it. I hope that this debacle will not permanently blight the future of the extreme travel community.

I hope that in years and decades to come this can be looked back on as a real exception to the general rule of honest dealings. It saddens me to think that, in the future, previously trusting travelers may be unwilling to accept offers at face value, or to trust one another with money; this will be William's legacy to a pursuit he was, truthfully, always passionate about, and he'll have to live with the shame of that poisoned legacy for the rest of his life."

Within hours of sending this message, William replied as follows:

Dear Mr. Seminara,

It would appear that you seem to know me much better than I know myself. So an interview would be superfluous.

Yours faithfully,
WILLIAM

I challenged William once more to address the final question in my letter. If he had done nothing wrong, why had his spokesperson written such an incriminating email to his creditors? Hours later, William wrote an email to Tim Wood and me:

> Hello Tim,
>
> Unlike many of the travellers, I have no intention to speak on behalf of others or what goes through their minds. Please help Mr. Seminara with his request, as it concerns something that you wrote in 2017. I am sure he would appreciate your expeditiousness.
>
> W.

Tim never responded. I waited nearly a month and sent William the following reply: "I never heard from Tim. But I have to say, acting as your spokesperson as you hid from all of your creditors must have been an extremely difficult job."

My short message apparently infuriated William because he sent me a nasty letter full of bible verses and threats to my family and me on April 4. In it, he referred to his extreme travel creditors as "defaulters" and "super defaulters," and he denied being in hiding, despite sending correspondence to me via Tim so I'd have no idea where he was. William quoted scripture to imply that COVID-19 was God's way of punishing horrible people like Harry Mitsidis and me:

> You can stay in your home, praying to be spared but The Lord has no shortage of ways

to forcibly break your quarantines. There is no place for you to run or hide when God is your pursuer. It is "As if a man did flee from a lion, and a bear met him; or went into the house, and leaned his hand on the wall, and a serpent bit him." (Amos 5:19). If it is your judgement time, He will not spare you or your wife or your sons from His fury.

I never told William anything about my sons, so this was creepy at very best or an outright threat at worst. And it got worse in the final paragraph:

We are all praying every day that the Lord will deliver his true judgement onto this rebellious and barren earth and it's [sic] inhabitants. We are all praying every day that He will deliver what is right and just unto you and your family, as well as the likes of [Harry] Mitsidis and others who live in sin, cursing and defacing the law of the Lord. God will stop at nothing when it comes to delivering what is just for you and your family. Covid-19 will strike like the sword of St. Michael through the ranks of the ungodly, as will many "disasters" yet to come.

He closed, ludicrously, with "kind regards" and a link to a YouTube video of a Johnny Cash song, "God's Gonna Cut You Down."

My first instinct was to tell him that I was going to hunt him down and beat his skinny carcass to a bloody pulp for wishing sickness, misfortune, or death upon my family members. Instead, I cooled off for a bit and sent him a measured response:

Reverend Gordon,

Please correct me if my interpretation of your message below is incorrect, Your Holiness. So you would like not just me but also my family members to become ill or perhaps die? And why is that? Because I've asked you questions in this email thread that you don't like?

This is indeed a time of reckoning for many people around the world. Rather than doubling down on old quarrels and grievances, some people are using the opportunity of this pandemic to view old problems in a new light. It's not up to me to inspire a detente between you and your extreme travel adversaries. But I'd love to see a happy ending to this saga. It would be wonderful to see you and the others reach a peaceful resolution that everyone can live with. I'm not sure anyone stands to benefit from a feud that has no end. Even the Hatfields and McCoy famil[y] in West Virginia and Kentucky eventually made peace.

I know there are several extreme travelers who are all hoping to get back on friendly terms

[with] you but I think they're waiting for an olive branch-- i.e. some admission of wrong-doing and an apology for any cancelled trips.

Of course you and Tim are under no obligation to answer my questions. The only reason I'm asking them is to give you a chance to provide any exculpatory information that you have. The point isn't to annoy you, it's to offer you an opportunity to set the record straight. These are examples of questions you could answer to help ensure that your side of the story is accurately reflected in my book.

1. Specific information on your Baekeland family lineage. (i.e. my great, great grandfather born in 1898 was George Baekeland and he was an uncle of Leo, etc. or whatever.)

2. You call your creditors your defaulters. I'd be happy to look at any evidence you have that would bolster this claim.

3. I know that you repaid Babis because he told me so. But if you've repaid other creditors, please tell me who they are so that I can say so in the book.

4. You say that you aren't in hiding but then why have the letters you sent me come through Tim and with no return address from you? So where are you now and are you making any travel plans or are you waiting to see what happens with COVID-19?

5.   I have done my best to reach out to as many extreme travelers as possible to get as many different perspectives in my story as possible. You've directed most of your bile in our correspondence toward 2 travelers: Harry and Dominique. I've interviewed quite a few travelers already but are there any whom you think might corroborate some elements of your side of the story? If so, let me know who they are and if I haven't already spoken to them, I will.

6.   You stated in one of your letters to me that you and your family were starting a church in Ireland. Has it opened?

> Despite the message you've sent me below, I do NOT wish ill health on you or your family. At a time like this, I think we should all be sending out positive vibes. So good luck, William, and do drop me a line if you are so inclined. If not, best wishes to you in your future endeavors.

> Dave Seminara

On April 10, William responded with a long email that failed to directly answer many of my questions. William rejected my suggestion that he consider apologizing to the travelers. He reiterated his dubious assertion that every country that investigated him has now dropped its investigation with no charges filed. And he audaciously insisted that Dominique Laurent and other travelers actually owe him money.

The young Brit declined to provide any evidence that he was a Baekeland or that he'd repaid any of his creditors. (He named one traveler that he claimed he had paid back and I attempted without success to verify his claim, as the traveler in question never responded.) And he claimed that his family's church in Ireland is now open, with five non-family member parishioners.

Finally, he claimed that he hadn't been wishing illness or death upon me and my family members in his previous message. "We are not p[r]aying for you and your family to become ill and die, we pray for the Lord to deliver his righteous judgement onto you, just as with everything else," he wrote. "I don't wish ill on you, I wish that you obey and live well."

❖   ❖   ❖

As William and I corresponded in March and April 2020, the COVID-19 virus morphed into a deadly pandemic that shook the world, and, for once, kept most travelers at home. But not William apparently. He told me in an April 10 email that he was still traveling, albeit for some unspecified business, not pleasure. "I have no moral qualms about travelling during this period, for the record," he wrote.

William didn't specify where he was but shortly after I received this message, I heard back from Jasmine, who claimed that William was in Bangui, Central African Republic. She said he was in the diamond business and had a large logging concession as well. "He also has a flat in Venice (Italy) but Venice is a no-go at the moment," she wrote.

Jasmine claimed that William had made "the most impactful decision of his life" in splitting with the family and their fledgling new church in Kildare, Ireland, over his bisexuality and other issues. She said he was raised in a strict Calvinist family who didn't approve of homosexuality. Jasmine wrote that he had, as he indicated to me earlier, been set to marry a woman, who was a longtime friend of his, in Italy. But it was called off after his mother and other family friends refused to attend for reasons she didn't detail.

"I don't know the full details really, or even most of the basics, but I'm pretty sure he is making a fortune out of it [the diamond business]," she wrote. "The church has no connection to this other than the tithe he used to give and I'm quite sure he didn't pay the 10% he should have."

I wondered about her motivations for sending me such messages and requested a phone interview. She agreed but never got in touch. Was this a poison pen letter from a relative who had had a falling-out with William?

Could the emails have been written by one of the angry travelers? Or perhaps they were written by William, hoping to throw me off his trail with the wildly improbable claim that he was living in the Central African Republic, a notoriously dangerous and corrupt place where one could easily be killed in the diamond trade?

By an unlikely coincidence, during my career in the Foreign Service, I was once the State Department's desk officer for the Central African Republic. I checked to see who the current U.S. ambassador in CAR was and was delighted to see it was Lucy Tamlyn, whom I had worked with during my time in State's Africa bureau. I sent her an email, asking her if she had seen William, who would absolutely stand out in a place like Bangui, which has few white expats. She replied quickly, confirming that there was no sign of him. Travelers I consulted didn't believe he was in Bangui. Perhaps Jasmine, or someone posing as Jasmine, was intentionally throwing me off his trail? Or perhaps William had told his family he was in Bangui and they believed it.

I may never know the truth, but when I sent William a draft copy of the book to read, he sent me the following reply (edited for the purposes of this book):

> Hi Dave,
>
> I have to say that I commend your effort for reaching out to Lisa St Aubin de Teran in Mozambique, although the assessment you both came to is wrong. What I was alluding to is not something that is possible to be known for a couple of decades (or perhaps a bit less). It is somewhat intangible, so the world can wait and see if they are curious (which I really doubt is the case…).
>
> As for the rest of the book, it is an interesting and well written book…There are quite a few minor mistakes in the book, many of them are simply unprovable though so there is little point in listing them out. A few of the ones which are completely provable also just seem completely trivial to me now at this stage. It would feel like flogging a dead horse as far as I'm concerned…
>
> It is a tired story and something that I no longer have any interest in thanks to Jigsaw (Productions) corporate stupidity. They dillied and dallied for months about a few minor contractual points and did not take me seriously when I told them that I won't take part unless

they can easily resolve them (which they had told me they would over the phone). As such, I withdrew just before filming. I have nothing to gain or lose from being in or out of their programme, and without me I am wondering what exactly they intend to do. I guess the logical solution is to turn it into the Harry and Dominique gossip show, which is something appropriate for them both and for this story in general...

The biggest issue that most people I face struggle to grasp (which included Jigsaw, and also you to an extent I think), is that I am just not interested in properly putting my case forward in a public setting. It is not something I can take seriously given the high-drama shown by those claiming to be creditors and, worse yet, "victims".

Kind regards,

William

Several weeks later, in late March 2021, I corresponded with William and asked him for an update.

"I do not wish to provide a significant update, although there is very little to say about the 'Great Matter,'" he wrote.

William said that he suffered culture shock after moving to North America at the end of Summer 2020. He declined to specify where and said that his mystery location has been "nice...if rather weird overall." He said that he's kept up a busy travel schedule during the pandemic, including (unspecified) business trips to the Central African Republic, South Sudan, Ethiopia, Zambia, and the United Arab Emirates.

He referenced attending a friend's wedding in Pakistan (five days long and with 3,000 people!) and visiting a host of remote islands with friends on a sports fishing boat, including Kingman Reef, Washington Island, Fanning Island, Malden Island, Starbuck Island, and Kiribati's Christmas Island (not Australia's where he sent me the Christmas card years before.)

"For an islophile, this is more than enough excitement and satisfaction to last some time," he wrote. "As for the rest of 2021…I expect another trip to Africa towards the end of summer, which I will combine with going back to Italy for a few weeks. Last year I was in Chad for a month and rather hope to explore a bit more of the Sahara this winter if possible, maybe Niger or Northern Mali— my itineraries for both of those are also month-long journeys."

William wrote that he had completed his book on Norwegian Antarctica but had shelved it because he would "feel like an imposter publishing it until (he) set foot on some Norwegian Antarctic territory."

He recounted his efforts to reach Bouvet Island with men he referred to as the "crazed TCC (Travelers' Century Club)" in "90 mph wind gusts."

"It (was) the closest atmosphere to a mutiny about to happen that I could imagine," he said. "Many loud passengers wanted to make an attempt (to land) come hell or high water. Some wanted to try to bribe the expedition staff to take the risk, one even wanted to jump overboard and swim. And a few wrote it off—as I did. No rock is worth that risk."

Perhaps not, but ever a man of many moods and contradictions, William admitted that he hadn't given up on Bouvet.

"I have a half-plan in the works to visit Bouvet in a couple of years with a few traveller friends so let us see what happens," he wrote.

He indicated that he plans to write a book detailing his thoughts on the "Great Matter." "I still maintain that reality is always less interesting than fiction and a lot of what has been put out there is fiction, or at least supposition and exaggeration."

He closed with an apology. "I would also like to apologize if any of my ramblings in the past have bothered you," he said. "My intention has always been to give you content and now you are weeks away from publishing so the purpose has been served. I will gladly remain in touch and look forward to hearing from you."

Our correspondence underscored my impression that William rather enjoyed being an international man of mystery. He probably relished sparring with me on some level and wasn't going to spoil the fun with direct answers to all of my questions. What's next for William? Dominique told me that a French prosecutor reviewing his case against William interviewed him for two hours in January 2021. But he wasn't optimistic he'd win in the courts.

"Justice in France is slow, bureaucratic, completely inefficient, politically oriented, and is often very mild towards criminals," he wrote in an email.

David Langan, the Irish super-traveler, sent me an email a week later to let me know that the Irish Gardai (police) had recently contacted him to follow up on leads after two years of silence. Nevertheless, I'd be surprised if any of the travelers beats William in the courts, and I'd be even more shocked if he was arrested.

I could be wrong but I don't see William as a con man in the classic sense of the term, though he clearly took advantage of the extreme travelers who trusted him. I think he's a wanderer who was interested in becoming an elite country collector. He wasn't impressed by some of the travelers who trusted and liked him but he sensed an opportunity and seized it. It's anyone's guess where he goes from here, but my bet is that it won't be one place but rather many, including plenty of the hard-to-reach variety.

❖   ❖   ❖

Many of the extreme travelers snuck in some bold trips right before the pandemic slammed borders shut around the globe. Gunther Holtorf, the German who travels rough had brought Otto II, his new truck, to Uruguay and promptly was stuck on a cattle farm their for two months. He finally got out of the country, but left Otto II behind and was waiting to get back to South America as this book was being published.

"Patience is the order of the day," he wrote.

Three dozen elite travelers met in late January for Kolja Spöri's annual Extreme Traveler International Congress in a remote chunk of Colombia that was formerly under FARC control. They had a blast and made it home safely before countries began closing their borders. And several others made a successful expedition to Chile's Desventuradas Island group—an MTP point that's five hundred miles off the coast.

A few of the travelers had traveled to Chile twice before based upon promises from William that he'd get them there but in each case, William had come up with creative excuses at the last moment, after they were already in country, to indefinitely postpone the voyages.

It was a week at sea, round trip, to reach the Desventuradas on a fifty-two-foot yacht, and a few of those days were in "better-carry-a-bucket" rough seas, but they made it at last, without William, and this was seen as a triumph.

Harry Mitsidis detailed his final trip—an eight-day jaunt in mid-March to South Sudan and Eritrea before the quarantine lockdown—in a NomadMania newsletter. Mitsidis described the pandemic as a "calamity for it attacks the very core of our being. The one thing we need more than anything, more than the air that we breathe, is freedom of movement, the ability to go and explore and be out there, doing our thing."

Mitsidis said that he considered whether it was ethical to go but elected to make the trip. "And so, hard as it was to fly on March 13 to Juba, not knowing what could happen and whether I may be stranded there, I did go for it, conscious of the fact that I am probably the last traveller of the season for both countries and with a deep feeling of guilt, even as I felt I was going to much safer places than anywhere in Europe and I thought at least I'm giving the locals, who will now suffer without any visitors, one last customer," he wrote.

Mitsidis bumped into fellow extreme traveler and Baekeland creditor Dominique Laurent by chance in Juba, and had a wonderful trip before returning to Europe on March 21. But he was haunted by questions haunting many of us: *When will I wake up in a hotel room again? When, in fact, will I get my next visa to a far-flung destination?*

The Greek-British super-traveler counseled all of us who are sad to be grounded to have some perspective and concluded his newsletter with some unlikely advice. "I never thought I would say this," he wrote, "but I guess I should: don't travel!"

But Kolja Spöri, another leader of the extreme travel movement, was having nothing of the #stayhome movement. On April 27, Spöri published an open letter to "former extreme travelers" in which he chided them for being brave enough to visit war zones but not to travel during the pandemic. The letter began as follows:

> Dear **former** Extreme Travelers,
>
> We cannot cross country borders for several months or more!
>
> The overreaction to a virus has destroyed the very essence that defines our little eco-system. Unfortunately, it came to my attention that we have a few among us who parrot official propaganda, like
> "stay together at home"
> "flatten the curve"
> "social distancing" and
> "masks save lives"

Spöri went on to rail against restrictions on travel, opining that the "current coronation of the virus, as a dictator over all humanity, is completely against the spirit of us 'extreme travelers', it is against our fundamental human rights, and against all known country constitutions – which were hard fought for by our ancestors, in order to protect us citizens from an abusive state! As bonafide extreme travelers, we must strongly protest the COVID-1984 regime, because it tramples on our highest values: the freedoms of movement and of association, among others."

The German extreme traveler continued, riffing on the many risks extreme travelers are willing to take. "We have inevitably dodged bullets in crime & conflict ridden countries on our bucket list…Can we really call ourselves 'extreme travelers', if we are not able to cope with the risk of a Common Flu anymore?"

Dominique Laurent said he agreed with Spöri 110 percent but Kolja told me that few travelers responded to his communiqué, leading him to believe that many extreme travelers were playing it safe and staying home.

But Spöri and other extreme travelers were more determined than ever to carry on, conquering their unvisited spots on various travel lists.

In August, while much of the world was still hunkered down in their homes, Spöri and eleven other top travelers made an expedition to Rockall Island, the huge uninhabited rock two hundred miles off the coast of Scotland. They braved force nine winds and twenty-foot waves, jumping off of Zodiac rafts with helmets on in order to swim to and touch the big rock. (As previously discussed, travelers cannot just see an island to count it as a legitimate visit, they must touch it and it's not possible to do this from a boat on Rockall due to the violent sea swells.) All but one of the travelers was able to touch Rockall and so the trip was considered a great success.

I was scheduled to take a Caribbean cruise in April, which was cancelled. And the pandemic hit America right around the time of year that I usually plan our family's big summer-long trip.

I looked at a global pandemic map and noted that many of the world's most dangerous countries—Somalia, Syria, CAR, and others—now seemed the safest, at least from COVID-19. But there was no way I could sell my wife on a family holiday to Mogadishu or Bangui, so I didn't even try. With borders closed around the world, I considered the fact that there are two U.S. states I've yet to visit: Oklahoma and North Dakota. But I knew there was no way I could sell my family on spending a summer holiday in either place. I had become a country collector, for better or worse.

While stuck at home one week in late March, I read Paul Theroux's take on the situation in the *New York Times*. He wrote, "The freedom that most travelers feel is often a delusion, for there is as much confinement in travel as liberation…in fact, most travel is a reminder of boundaries and limits."

For a moment, I thought he was ready to conclude that perhaps travel was overrated. This from a man who has extolled the pleasures of travel for nearly fifty years. Perhaps Theroux, now eighty, was rethinking his lifelong passion for travel? Apparently, not so much. He concludes at the end of the piece that the most "enlightening" trips he's taken have also been "the riskiest, the most crisis-ridden." "We are living in just such a moment of risk…this crisis makes me want to light out for the territory ahead of the rest. It would be a great shame if it were not somehow witnessed and documented."

I should have been looking at the big picture—I'm on three immunity-suppressing drugs and my parents are in their eighties and living in a retirement home in Western New York. We were all in good shape, bored as hell, but still alive. The pandemic could have been a reminder that there are more important things in life than travel, but it was hard to see that big picture through my novelty-seeking sunglasses.

I traded emails with Harry Mitsidis in April and he reminded me that I had yet to fill out my travel resume on his NomadMania website. I procrastinated completing my list because I knew that my ranking would be pitiful. But the quarantine boredom provided the perfect opportunity to sit down and finally work on my list. It took nearly two hours to recall not just what countries but also what regions I've visited in my decades as a traveler.

When I finished my list, I clicked on my personal travel map. The chunks of the world I've visited were lit up in red but huge swathes of the planet remained grayed out. My stats were mediocre at best: 293 spots visited on Harry's list of 1,281 places, 224 places out of 949 on Charles Veley's MTP list, and 84 places out of 329 on the TCC list. My NomadMania ranking was a paltry #841 overall and #186 among American travelers.

The State Department was advising Americans against leaving the country. Nations around the world had closed their borders to foreign visitors. Perhaps the virus was a test and those of us who couldn't resist the siren call of the road would get sick or die. And yet, oddly enough, the allure of places I've never visited felt stronger than ever before. I got my second dose of the Pfizer vaccine on April 1, 2021, and left for the Dominican Republic, my first international destination in more than seventeen months, the very next day. I realized that, for better or worse, I'm a mad traveler, just like the rest.

ACKNOWLEDGMENTS

◇◇◇◇◇◇◇◇◇◇◇◇◇◇◇◇

Massive thanks, as always, to my wife, Jen, and my sons, Leo and James, for their encouragement and good cheer. Thanks to my parents and my brothers for being fans of my work.

This book unfolded over a period of several years and I had help from so many travelers. Thanks to everyone who took the time to speak with me for this book. I'm not going to name every single source here, as some requested anonymity, but you know who you are.

I owe a large debt of gratitude to some of my friends who read portions of this book: Tom Swick, Georgi Filipovski, Dan Boylan, Megan Fernandez, and Deirdre Carney. And a golem extra thanks to Georgi Filipovski for helping me format this manuscript.

ABOUT THE AUTHOR

Author photo by Todd Burgess

Dave Seminara is a writer, former diplomat, and pathological traveler who lives in St. Petersburg, Florida. His writing has appeared in *The New York Times*, which first published a brief account of this journey, *The Wall Street Journal*, BBC, *The Washington Post*, and dozens of other publications. He is the author of *Footsteps of Federer: A Fan's Pilgrimage Across 7 Swiss Cantons in 10 Acts* and two other books: *Bed, Breakfast & Drunken Threats: Dispatches from the Margins of Europe* and *Breakfast with Polygamists: Dispatches from the Margins of The Americas*.